T0289001

BOXING SHADOWS

BOXING SHADOWS

By W. K. Stratton
with Anissa "The Assassin" Zamarron

UNIVERSITY OF TEXAS PRESS ◆ AUSTIN

The publication of this book was made possible by a contribution from Richard Garriott and Anne Stilwell Strong.

Requests for permission to reproduce material from this work should be sent to:
    Permissions
    University of Texas Press
    P.O. Box 7819
    Austin, TX 78713-7819
    www.utexas.edu/utpress/about/bpermission.html

♾ The paper used in this book meets the minimum requirements of ANSI/NISO Z39.48-1992 (R1997) (Permanence of Paper).

Library of Congress Cataloging-in-Publication Data

Stratton, W. K.
Boxing shadows / by W. K. Stratton with Anissa "The Assassin" Zamarron. — 1st ed.
    p.   cm.
ISBN 978-0-292-72129-6 (cloth : alk. paper)
1. Zamarron, Anissa.   2. Boxers (Sports)—United States—Biography.
3. Women boxers—United States—Biography.   I. Title.
GV1132.Z36S87   2009
796.83092—dc22
[B]

2009015033

Boxing is not just about throwing blows, it's about learning. You have to learn to adapt, to adjust in the ring. You're successful because you work hard and believe in what you do. . . . When you fall, you have to get up and go again, go again. It's how you recover from that trouble. . . . A great fighter knows what survival is about.

—JOHNNY CASAS, WELTERWEIGHT BOXER

I can entertain the proposition that life is a metaphor for boxing—for one of those bouts that go on and on, round following round, jabs, missed punches, clinches, nothing determined, again the bell and again and you and your opponent so evenly matched it's impossible not to see that your opponent is you. . . . Life is like boxing in many unsettling respects.

—JOYCE CAROL OATES, "ON BOXING"

CONTENTS

ACKNOWLEDGMENTS

B ecause it is her story, *Boxing Shadows* is based primarily on the recollections of Anissa, told from her point of view. In addition, supplementary interviews were conducted with some of the people who are a part of her story. The authors also used information gathered from a number of publications, including *Texas Monthly, Sports Illustrated, Esquire, The Ring Magazine,* the *New York Times,* the *Los Angeles Times,* the *Washington Post,* the *Miami Herald,* the *San Antonio Express-News,* the *Fort Worth Star-Telegram,* the *Austin American-Statesman,* the *Dallas Morning News,* and the *Houston Chronicle.* Several Internet Web sites provided helpful information, especially the Women Boxing Archive Network (WBAN). While working on her PhD at the University of Texas, Benita Anitta Heiskanen, a citizen of Finland, trained at Richard Lord's Boxing Gym in Austin. Her dissertation, "Fighting Bodies: The Body in Space and Place," focused largely on Latino and Latina boxers and provided insightful information for *Boxing Shadows,* as did her article "On the Ground and Off: The Theoretical Practice of Professional Boxing," which appeared in *The European Journal of Cultural Studies.*

We appreciate the enthusiasm and, frankly, patience of the staff of the University of Texas Press. We especially want to thank our editor, Allison Faust, who has guided this project from the beginning with determination and a deft hand. We also want to thank Dave Hamrick and Theresa J. May for their roles in opening the doors for *Boxing Shadows* at UT Press.

It goes without saying we are greatly indebted to Richard and

Lori Lord, their family, and the patrons of Richard Lord's Boxing Gym for their support of this project. Richard also was generous enough to provide photographs for the book. We also are thankful to Richard Garriott for his support and for use of his photographs.

We want to express our deep debt to Dr. Ted Spears, his wife, Rita, and their family, as well as the staff at Sports Performance International in Austin. Dr. Spears has performed surgery on both authors in order to keep them active, but beyond that, he graciously allowed us to use the conference room at Sports Performance International to record Anissa's recollections. We recorded many hours of tape on Sunday afternoons and lunch hours during workdays in that conference room, and those tapes form the heart of *Boxing Shadows*. Moreover, the Spears family has been a steady source of support and counsel—not to mention employment—for Anissa over the past few years. This proved especially valuable as she revisited some of the darkest corners of her life as the book took shape.

We also want to say thanks to Linda McFall, who did a terrific job of transcribing our many tapes during challenging times for her and her family. We want to thank David Marion Wilkinson, Jan Reid, Jesse Sublett, and Christopher Cook for their helpful suggestions. And, finally, our thanks to Kevin Stark, Anissa's longtime friend and supporter and, especially, our thanks to Anissa's family for their support and understanding.

BLOOD

In her darkest days, before her life took direction, she lay pinned to a bed under a Posey net, which stretched from her neck to her feet, with leather cuffs for the upper arms, wrists, and ankles and cross-straps securing all the binding to the sides of the bed. The restraints prevented her from cutting herself, so she mastered biting the insides of her mouth until her blood flowed. That was one thing that gave her a high, seeing her own blood. The Posey net never stayed clean for very long. Soon it would be caked with her blood and soaked with her urine. Naturally, the bed and the net reeked. She stank, too. The techs didn't seem to care. As she lay bound to the bed, they'd leave her in the same bra for months on end and eventually there'd be layers of dead skin under it. And she had bedsores, just like a geriatric patient in a substandard nursing home who seldom gets turned in bed. No one cut her hair and it now crept all the way down to her waist, ratty and filthy: witch's hair. Because she couldn't move her feet, skin grew over her toenails. But none of that seemed to be a big deal to the staff at the hospital.

And so she lay there, trapped and scheming—scheming about ways to hurt the people who were doing this to her. And scheming about ways to hurt herself.

BOXING SHADOWS

CHAPTER ONE

It hurts to box. People look at you and say, "Well, you're
in shape, you're ready to box." It's more than that though.

—ANISSA

. . . . .

A rambunctious San Antonio fight crowd turned out for the
card at the Roseland Ballroom that November night in
2005. The venue is situated in the Estrella Mall in the shade of an
Interstate highway junction in a rather nondescript section of the
Alamo City. Anissa Zamarron, a former world champion boxer,
was not impressed by the ballroom and the surrounding area. In
fact, it seemed pretty shabby to her. But that's how it is in women's
boxing. Championship fights often occur in settings far removed
from the glitz associated with, say, top-flight women's tennis or ice
skating competitions.

Indeed, tonight a world title was on the line at Roseland Ballroom. At thirty-five, Anissa would be entering the ring against
the talented hometown favorite, Maribel Zurita, who was nearly a
decade younger than Anissa. They had fought twice before in close
matches, and Anissa had scored victories in both meetings. Yet it
was Zurita who currently held the Women's International Boxing Association's world junior flyweight (108 pounds) title, which
she had captured three months earlier by defeating Japanese boxer
Sachiyo Shibata in a fight at San Antonio's Municipal Audito-
rium—it was the first women's world championship boxing match
held in the city.

Anyone betting on the fight had to consider Zurita the clear
favorite, never mind Anissa's earlier victories against her. Zurita's

career was ascending, while Anissa had just lost four fights in a row. In those fights, Anissa had seemed to be a mere shadow of the boxer she'd once been. Her lifetime ring record had fallen to 16-14-2. Friends concerned about her physical well-being began to whisper behind her back that she should retire before she suffered serious injury in the ring. If not for her health, their reasoning went, she should quit before she frittered away her winning career record, since she now had only two more victories than defeats.

Anissa, too, understood the precariousness of where her career stood. After her last defeat, she realized she was going to have to train harder and bring renewed focus to the ring if she were going to compete at the highest level of her sport. One good thing about this fight was that she'd had extra time to prepare for it. She'd not fought since March, which meant she had been training for nearly eight months.

"I'd never before trained as hard for a fight as I did for this one," Anissa says. "I'd been introduced to a trainer, Andy Pastran, and over the past few months he'd really kicked my butt to get me ready. I'm the sort of athlete who always likes to push beyond the limits whenever I'm training, and Andy always made me do more than I thought I could do. He had been brutal with me. And I loved it."

She combined Andy's ring-focused work on fundamentals with the always challenging physical conditioning regimen laid down by her regular trainer and manager, Richard Lord: running on the Hike and Bike Trail at Town Lake (soon to be renamed Lady Bird Lake) in downtown Austin five times a week, early morning weight training at Hyde Park Gym three times a week, sparring with other female boxers on Saturday mornings, workouts at Richard's boxing gym every day on heavy, speed, and double-end punching bags. And, every Sunday at eight A.M. sharp, she joined with Richard and his hard-core acolytes, including other professional boxers, to run the ramps at Darrell K Royal Texas Memorial Stadium on the University of Texas campus.

Running the ramps is a particularly grueling part of Richard's training plan. The ramps, which accommodate fans walking to their seats when the Longhorns are at home for football, switch-back their way up the west side of the stadium for eleven stories. Running these ramps from the ground to their peak would be challenging enough. But Richard introduces a few twists to make it even more difficult, as Anissa explains: "We do it in an up-and-down cycle that goes like this: You run up the first ramp, stop, and return to the bottom. Then you run to the top of the second ramp, stop, and return to the bottom. You keep on like that until you've followed that up-and-down pattern until you reach the end of the eleventh ramp. Then you reverse it: From the ground you run to the top of the eleventh level, then all the way back to the bottom; run to the top of the tenth level, then all the way back to the bottom. And so on. And you run it as fast as you can.

"It's brutal stuff. Every muscle in your lower body aches. But the really hard part is putting your mind in the right place so that you can continue and get it done. About halfway through, your mind starts telling you that you can't continue, that you have to stop. But you have to overcome that. I think running the ramps is very important because when you're in a ten-round boxing match, there will come a point where your mind says you have to stop, that you just can't take any more. Running the ramps teaches you how to deal with that."

Another important lesson comes from running the ramps: Lord himself is the one who usually completes the drill the quickest, even though he is in his fifties. The people he trains are in their twenties and thirties for the most part. No one needs to say it out loud, but the message is clear: If the old man is able to do this as efficiently as he does, his younger charges should be able to find it within themselves to keep up. The routine is extremely difficult to complete. First-timers are known to plunge their legs in five-gallon buckets of ice water after the drill in an attempt to squelch at least some of the searing pain guaranteed to assault the calf muscles over the next twenty-four hours.

In addition to the physical workouts, Anissa also had been adhering to a strict diet that eliminated candy and other sweets, sodas, and fried foods. Instead she focused on vegetables and fruits, whole grains, lean poultry, and fish. Anissa came to view her body as something like a high-performance automobile: When you have a brand-new Mercedes, she would say, you don't burn regular in it—you fill it with premium. Likewise, she fueled her body with premium food. The one treat she allowed herself actually enhanced her training. Another trainer with whom she'd worked, the talented Flaco Castrejon, who had relocated to the Austin area from Mexico City to work with her friend, two-time world champion Jesus Chavez, recommended she drink a beer—a single beer—to help "kill the edge you get from so much training." That beer at the end of the day also helped her sleep. Boxers tend to need more sleep than most people because, as Anissa would say, "you beat the crap out of your body all day, you have to sleep to allow it to repair itself." So the beer was both a treat and a means to help her recover from her workouts.

Anissa arrived in San Antonio well conditioned, well trained, and well rested. She wasn't sure what the future held for her as a prizefighter, wasn't sure if she would win this fight. But she believed she had the preparation to do something she'd never accomplished in the dozen years that had passed since her first pro boxing match: fight at the very best of her ability. When she mentally replayed her thirty-one previous ring outings, she always was able to find defects in her performance. Those things, both little and big, that she could have done better haunted her. Before she walked away from the ring, she wanted to have one fight about which she could say she did everything as well as she possibly could.

In some ways, that had become even more important than notching a win.

. . . . .

Going into fight week, Anissa had followed the rituals she'd adhered to over the course of her long ring career. She'd tapered off on training to give her body time to rest and recover from the grueling workouts she'd been enduring; a successful boxer has to feel fresh and energized when she steps into the ring on fight night. She continued to eat light, nutritious meals. She made sure to get plenty of sleep. She did all she could to avoid stress and other kinds of emotional distractions; a boxer has to be focused if she is going to succeed.

On the day of the fight, she slept late, then had a breakfast of oatmeal — "good, slow-burning carbs." She took a long walk to let her food digest. Later, she had a light lunch of roasted chicken and potatoes. And she began her usual fight day routine for hydration.

Throughout her career, Anissa tried to keep her weight close to the mark she needed to hit for the weigh-in, which usually occurs a day before the fight. One criticism Anissa has of male fighters in general is that they seem to be more careless than female fighters at controlling their weight and therefore are involved in tough battles to cut weight prior to a weigh-in. But even a boxer like Anissa who tries to keep her weight under control will scale back on food and water on the day of the weigh-in, if not for two or three days before. Once the boxer has made weight, she'll then embark on rehydrating herself and replenishing electrolytes.

Anissa began her rehydration ritual that morning with a bottle of Gatorade. After she emptied the bottle, she refilled it with water and drank that. She kept refilling and drinking throughout the day. By dusk, her weight stood at close to 115 pounds, 7 pounds more than she'd registered at the weigh-in. All that water made her feel like she was going to explode, not to mention that she was urinating every time she turned around, yet she kept drinking, knowing she'd sweat away, during the ten rounds of the fight, all 7 pounds she'd gained.

Between trips to the water fountain and trips to the bathroom, Anissa tried to relax and nap a little. She left any issues that arose to Richard Lord to resolve, knowing she could trust him to take care of things. One of the worst things that could happen to Anissa—or any boxer—in the hours leading up to a fight was to get mentally distracted.

At six P.M., she, Lord, and Jesus Chavez, who along with Richard would be working Anissa's corner that night, checked in at the Roseland Ballroom. It was Anissa's first time to fight in San

Antonio, which is a little surprising, given that San Antonio is a hot boxing town and Anissa had spent her career of more than thirty fights based just ninety miles away in Austin. After checking in, she decided she hadn't missed much by not fighting there.

She discovered she would be using an office for a locker room. There were no mirrors in the room, just a desk, a couple of chairs, and a blackboard. She did find a shower in the women's restroom, which was a relief: At least she'd be able to take a shower after her fight. But so far she concluded that the San Antonio promoters were living up to the reputation they had among the boxers she knew: They, like their counterparts in Houston, would try to do everything as cheaply as possible, cutting corners wherever they saw them. Because of that, Anissa had opted for a cash advance from the promoters rather than accepting a paid-for motel room of their choosing. She'd heard too many stories about boxers being stuck in fleabag lodgings alongside a noisy Interstate highway.

As the featured fighters on the card, Anissa and Zurita would be the last boxers to enter the ring that evening, so there was no rush for her to get ready. As the preliminary bouts got under way, she found her mother and her brother, Roland. In the years since she took up boxing, Roland had been her biggest fan, saving every scrap of paper containing anything written about one of his sister's fights and traveling to be at her fights in person if at all possible or watching them on TV or over the Internet when he couldn't. Before each fight, he made a point of finding his kid sister and telling her, "No matter what happens out there, we still love you." Whenever Anissa heard those words, she felt a lot of the prefight stress slide off her shoulders. And after each fight he and Anissa went through a standard routine:

Roland: Who's number one?
Anissa: Me!
Roland: Who's the champ?
Anissa: Me!
Roland: Who loves you?
Anissa: You!

Regardless of the outcome of the bout, this ritual always made Anissa feel good. Also, before a fight, Roland would open his house up to Anissa to provide her a sanctuary away from telephone calls and other distractions. Whatever success she enjoyed during her boxing career, she attributed a good part of it to the support of her brother.

As she talked to Roland and her mother, she learned that the ballroom did not offer beer for sale, which astonished both of them. Beer goes with prizefighting as much as it does with a major league baseball game. Ever resourceful, they had discovered a workaround for the dry situation. Down the street was a gas station that sold beer, so Anissa's mother walked there and bought beer in cans, which they poured into paper cups. Then they walked back to the ballroom, cups of beer in hand. This inspired other fans.

"You should see it," Roland said. "There's a whole line of people out there going down to the gas station and another line of people coming back the opposite direction to the ballroom."

They all had a good laugh. Then Anissa went back to her make-shift locker room. Along the way, she saw Zurita with her manager, Tony Ayala.

. . . . .

Given the close outcome of their two previous fights, Texas fans of women's boxing had come to consider Anissa and Zurita as rivals. There were plenty of side elements to make the rivalry appealing. Anissa was the older fighter, a former world champion; Zurita, the hungry up-and-comer who'd just claimed her first world title. The geographical rivalry between the two fighters' hometowns—Austin and San Antonio—figured into it as well, given that the cities are just an hour and a half's drive apart. And something of a rivalry existed between the two managers involved, Lord and Ayala, each arguably the best-known manager/trainer in his respective city.

Anissa held no strong feelings toward Zurita one way or another—"I don't really even know her. I think she'll be a great person to get to know once all this bullshit is done"—but Ayala was a different matter. A distinguished-looking man with a distinctive white mane of hair, Ayala was a familiar figure to Texas boxing fans. People who follow the sport also saw him frequently on national television in the 1980s when his son, Tony Jr., billed by some as the best prospect in boxing history, tore through nearly two dozen straight victories before a rape conviction brought his career as a contender to an end. Tony Sr. was Tony Jr.'s manager and trainer. In San Antonio, Tony Sr. operated a downtown gym, credited by many in the community with keeping poor kids off the street. He always fielded dominant teams in Texas amateur boxing competitions, often featuring his sons; indeed, Tony Jr. and his brothers Sammy and Mike all won national Golden Gloves titles, the only trio of brothers to pull off such a feat. Anissa's friend Jan Reid wrote in *Texas Monthly:* "To some Chicanos, Tony Sr. has earned . . . esteem and affection for the credit he brought to their young people and the city of San Antonio. But to others, it is an article of faith that the Ayala boys succeeded in the ring because their father raised them like pit bulls."

Ayala was never shy about bulldogging the press whenever he felt one of his fighters came up on the wrong end of ring judges' decisions. After Anissa's second victory over Zurita, he told *San Antonio Express-News* writer John Whisler, "Maribel beat this girl from pillar to post. Something's got to be done, man, this is terrible." Ayala's attempts to discredit Anissa as a fighter in print left her with a less than high opinion of the man. She also saw a measure of hypocrisy in him. When women's boxing began to bloom in earnest in the 1980s and early '90s, Ayala had been a vocal critic of women in the ring. Yet by the early 2000s, his most successful professional fighter was female.

Anissa knew that focusing on her personal feelings about Ayala—or about anyone else, for that matter—was the kind of thing that could disrupt her concentration for the fight, maybe get her into trouble. So she didn't let her mind wander in that direction. When the first bout of the evening got under way, Richard said to her, "Okay, let's wrap up."

Anissa nodded and held a hand up to him, fingers outstretched. It had become pretty much a ritual for Richard to wrap her hands during the first fight on the card. Against the muffled shouts of the fans, Richard webbed gauze and medical tape over and around her knuckles and her fingers. It's a job a trainer must do carefully, primarily because the wraps are the fundamental protection a boxer has against breaking her knuckles or fingers when she hits her opponent. Also, the wraps will be inspected by a state official to ensure they have not been layered with an object or a substance that might give a boxer an unfair advantage, just as her boxing gloves will be inspected as well. Slipping a horseshoe into a boxing glove prior to a fight seems like a gag from a 1940s Warner Bros. cartoon, but the fact is that wrap and glove doctoring sometimes occurs in real life. One example: Boxer Luis Resto acknowledged in the 2008 documentary *Cornered* that the tape used to wrap his hands had been soaked in plaster of Paris prior to his ten-round fight with Billy Collins Jr. in 1983. His trainers also removed two inches of padding from each of his gloves, so every blow struck on Collins was essentially nothing but fist and hardened plaster. Collins, who died in a car wreck nine months later, never recovered from the injuries he received that night.

Her hands secured in their wraps, Anissa put on her headphones and listened to music while concentrating on the task before her. As always before a fight, she found herself in a paradoxical situation: It was important to focus on the fight and what she would have to do to win it, but it was equally as important for her to try to be as calm as possible. "You're nervous," she says, "and you're still peeing a lot. A lot of things go through your head about your opponent. You wonder what she's been doing to get ready for this fight, how much she's improved, whether she has any new little tricks." At the weigh-in, Anissa had looked Maribel over, attempting to judge what kind of shape she might be in (she appeared to be in top form) and pondered whether she'd had any trouble making weight—a boxer who struggles to make weight often enters the ring the next day feeling weak. Those thoughts came back to Anissa now as she waited for her turn in the ring. "You always think a lot before a fight, especially wondering if tonight's going to be your night. All that worrying and thinking—it's really just nervous energy, I guess. Sometimes a less experienced fighter can also fret about all the worrying she's doing, which makes everything even worse. One advantage I had that night was that I'd been in enough fights to know everything was going to be okay once I climbed into the ring. Still, I couldn't help but wonder how much Maribel had improved since the last time we fought."

At the start of the card's third fight, Anissa put on her boxing shoes. The shoes look something like work boots, with uppers that lace high above the ankles to provide protection for the joint. But they are much, much lighter, with thin, flat soles to accommodate a boxer's need to pivot. Tonight her shoes were black. She also would wear a black sports bralike top and black trunks with ANISSA spelled out in silver across the front of the waistband. She slipped into her fight attire during the card's intermission, with two or three preliminary fights remaining before the main event.

She began warming up, loosening up slowly, rising up on the balls of her feet, shifting her weight from foot to foot, shadowboxing a little. Suddenly Richard appeared.

"The fight going on right now isn't going to last very long," he said. "We need to get you ready."

He reached for a container of Vaseline, then began to smear the petroleum jelly on Anissa's face—a standard practice for boxers to provide protection from abrasions from their opponents' gloves. Richard next tied on her gloves. Then he dug through a bag until he found a pair of mitts, which he put on his own hands. Mitts are thick pads with a glovelike attachment on the back; in a way, each resembles a catcher's mitt. Mitts are elemental tools for training boxers. A trainer holds the mitts in various positions and calls out combinations to the boxer. The boxer responds by slamming her gloves into the mitts in correspondence to the combination. Mitt workouts are vigorous, and soon Anissa had broken a sweat. She was ready to go into the ring. The timing was good, for soon a run-

ner appeared to announce that it was time for the boxers to make
their entrance.

With music thudding loudly over the PA system, Anissa entered
the ring first. Zurita, as champion, followed shortly thereafter. The
level of applause let Anissa know that while this was a pro-Zurita
crowd, there also was a loud contingent of her own fans from
Austin present.

. . . . .

When the bell rang to start their fight in San Antonio, Zurita
came out banging, *boom-boom-boom!* Earlier in the evening, there
had been a bout with two female boxers, both of whom were inexperienced compared to Anissa and Zurita. Their fight had been
relatively lackluster and no doubt lowered crowd expectations for
the next female bout. So the fast and furious exchange of blows in
the first round of Anissa and Zurita's fight surprised the audience
and immediately brought it to its feet. A loud chant of *Ma-ri!*
Ma-ri! Ma-ri! resounded from the San Antonio partisans. But the
large group of Anissa's fans became vocal as well, and their cheers
for Anissa soon competed with the *Ma-ri!* chants.

Zurita's strategy became clear during that first round. She and
Ayala, who was working her corner, must have believed that Zurita, the younger fighter by a decade, would come into the ring
with more energy and stamina than Anissa. So, if Zurita pressed
Anissa hard and fast in the early going, she would collapse under
the onslaught. Anissa admits that in her first two fights with Zurita, her conditioning was nowhere near peak level, and she believes
Ayala saw that as her vulnerability. Ayala and Zurita's strategy
would have been sound had Anissa not worked harder preparing
for this fight than for any other in her career. She was in the best
shape of her life. Though Zurita's attack surprised her, she adjusted
quickly.

Anissa says, "I thought, 'Okay, if that's how you want to go at
it, I know how to do this.' And I started banging right back at her.

It was crazy, nonstop punching from both of us. In round two, she came out banging again, and I banged right back at her. There was no way I was going to run out of gas like I did the first two fights. The third round was pretty much the same thing.

"In boxing, we say that a world championship fight doesn't really start until the fourth round. A championship fight is not just another fight. It's all nerves and willpower, and you just don't know how things are going to turn out during those early rounds. But one thing you do know is that what matters is how you finish up. The judges base a lot on who finishes the strongest, who is 'there' at the end of the fight. I've been told that I've fought more ten-round fights—in women's boxing, title fights last ten rounds—than any woman in history. I don't know how you prove that, but I can say I don't know of any woman who has fought more than I have. I've been in enough of them to know that what matters in terms of the decision is which boxer can take the fight all the way through to the end. And who is going to be able to take it all the way through begins to show in the fourth round."

Sure enough, Anissa noticed that Zurita slowed down a little in the fourth round. Anissa threw a straight right that connected hard to Zurita's chin and Zurita staggered backward toward the ropes. Anissa couldn't tell if Zurita was off-balance because of the blow itself or if she'd tripped over her own feet while backing out of the "pocket"—that is, where a boxer is standing close enough to her opponent to be able to hit her. Anissa was momentarily confused. If Zurita was unsteady on her feet because of the blow, she should go into full attack mode and pummel Zurita, hoping to score at least a knockdown if not a knockout. On the other hand, if Anissa attacked Zurita who was unsteady because she stumbled on her own feet, the referee could charge Anissa with a foul. Her position in the ring didn't allow her to see the referee and she could not really tell what was happening with Zurita. So, in that split second, Anissa opted to do what she thought was prudent. She held back. She learned that she legitimately had Zurita in trouble only at the end of the round, when Richard and Chavez chastised her in the corner for not sticking it to her opponent when she had the chance. "To tell the truth," Anissa says, "I didn't know what was happening. I didn't know if I legally could go across the ring and smack her, although now I know I should have jumped on her. So Maribel stayed on her feet and there was no knockdown."

Worse from Anissa's perspective, Ayala had a chance to revive Zurita with water and ice as she sat on a stool in her corner for the minute of rest between rounds four and five. Zurita came back throwing down hard in the fifth round, although she lacked some of the aggression she'd shown in the earlier rounds. Anissa saw Zurita breathing with her mouth slightly open: a sign of fatigue in the boxing ring. Moreover, a boxer fighting with her mouth open is risking a broken jaw, since she's sacrificing the protection provided by clamping down on her mouthpiece with her lips sealed. Anissa tried to exploit what she read as a weakness in Zurita. But Maribel proved to be resilient, showing a toughness Anissa had not seen in earlier fights with her. Anissa went to the corner between rounds wondering how much longer Zurita could keep this up. And a small part of Anissa fretted about how long she herself could continue.

"You got to stop brawling with her," Richard said in the corner.

"Box her," Jesus implored as he splashed water over her mouthpiece. "If you want to win this, you have to box her."

The message rang true. She and Zurita had been in a slugfest through the early rounds, throwing punch after punch. Anissa's best strategy was to start employing the classic elements of boxing, showing the sweet science of the sport as opposed to brawling. There's an old adage that holds that the boxer will defeat the brawler every time. Maybe so. What is true (at least most of the time) is that the boxer looks better to the judges scoring the fight. Boxing rather than brawling would win her rounds.

Anissa began employing the fundamentals she'd worked so hard on with Andy. Sticking and moving. Throwing combinations. Feint, feint, slip, slip. Counterpunching. Keeping better control of the ring with her foot movement. And above all, staying busy.

"I boxed the shit out of her, to tell the truth," Anissa remembers, "although there were some rounds that made me wonder if I'd done enough to impress the judges. I kept busy, staying inside as much as possible, scoring, *pow-pow-pow!* Now the crowd can't really see a lot of this. A lot of the scoring goes on inside where only the referee and the judges at ringside have a good view. I'm sure a lot of the people in the crowd thought Maribel was winning because she was the hometown girl and she was still throwing and looking impressive. But I knew I was scoring a lot when I got in the pocket and started delivering."

But she had no idea how much of this had registered with the judges when the bell rang to end the tenth round. One thing was certain: The crowd loved the show she and Zurita had given them. The fans were on their feet and the San Antonio partisans started up their deafening *Ma-ri! Ma-ri! Ma-ri!* chant again. It reminded Anissa that she was on Zurita's turf. Usually the champ wins the benefit of the doubt in boxing matches determined by decision instead of a knockout or technical knockout. This is especially true when the champ has the benefit of homecookin': fighting in her hometown with judges selected by a hometown promoter. In most cases a local champion has to be beaten convincingly in order for her to lose her title belt.

While the uncertainty of the decision vexed her during those long moments in the ring as the judges tallied their scorecards, it dawned on her that she had just accomplished something significant—at least for her. She'd never performed in the ring quite like she had tonight. If she'd brawled during the early rounds, it was because that was the appropriate response to Zurita's onslaught. She made adjustments as the fight went on, letting her boxing skills come to the forefront in the later rounds. True, she had not pursued Zurita when she was in trouble in the fourth round, but that had been a judgment call, and a correct one, given the circumstances. Better to exercise restraint than to act rashly and incur a penalty that could affect the outcome of the scoring. Whatever the judges' decision might be, Anissa had notched a victory for herself. She'd just fought the best fight of her career.

Against the crowd pandemonium, the announcer collected the

judges' scorecards. She could see Zurita's fans were already celebrating. Even though the roar from the audience made conversation impossible, Anissa somehow heard Richard say to her, "I don't care what happens with the decision. You did a great job." Then he repeated it: "You did a great job."

Finally the ring announcer stepped up to the microphone and called the boxers and their seconds to the center of the ring. The crowd grew quiet as he delivered the decision: "Judge Roy Ovalle scores the fight 97-93 for Maribel Zurita." Wild applause erupted briefly from the Zurita fans. "Judge Anthony Townsend scores it 96-94 for Anissa Zamarron." Now cheers came from the fans of Anissa mixed with a few boos from the San Antonians. "Judge Joel Elizondo scores the fight 97-93 for the winner . . . and *new* WIBA world junior flyweight champion, Anissa Zamarron!"

Jeers and cheers competed with each other from the crowd, but Anissa felt overwhelmed. She'd done it. She was world champion again. A photograph from that night captures her emotions. The referee lifts her hand to designate her as the winner. Anissa's other hand shoots up and she is standing on the balls of her feet. Her mouth is open, an expression of stunned disbelief on her face. Zurita, on the other hand, is registering her own sort of disbelief. She is staring up at the ceiling, a look of I-can't-believe-this-is-happening-again forged on her face. Anissa says, "I just went, 'Holy shit!'" That shocked, holy shit feeling stayed with her for a month.

But the decision stirred controversy, at least among the San Antonio fans, as soon as it was announced, and controversy continued for days to come. At ringside shortly after the bout's conclusion, Zurita told a reporter that she didn't know what fight the judges were watching. "It was a good fight, but I thought I landed the stronger, harder punches. I'm very disappointed." In the days that followed, rumors circulated in San Antonio that the fight had been fixed. The hullabaloo became substantial enough that San Antonio sportswriter John Whisler devoted a column in the *Express-News* to it. Had he been a judge, Whisler wrote, he would have given the decision to Zurita, although he added that with the number of punches thrown, several of the rounds could have been scored in favor of either boxer. "Conspiracy theorists might not like that conclusion any more than they liked the judges' scorecards that night. There were some unusual circumstances that clouded an unpopular decision. But there were no attempts to deceive or manipulate the outcome. It was the good, the bad, and the ugly of the sport all in the same night. It was controversial. But it wasn't corrupt. In short, it was just boxing."

The conspiracy theory storm centered around the two judges who ranked Anissa as the winner on their scorecards, Townsend and Elizondo. The conspiracy theorists mentioned in Whisler's column claimed that Townsend, who is from Austin, had been one of Richard Lord's fighters and thus would have been inclined to show favoritism to Anissa. In fact, Townsend was associated with a competing gym in Austin. "When he was a fighter, he lost to a couple of kids from my gym," Lord told Whisler. "When I heard he was one of the judges, I was worried he'd be biased against us."

As for Joel "World Famous" Elizondo, it was true that he and Jesus Chavez were friends, and it was true that he had sparred a few times at Lord's gym in Austin. It was also true that Lord never trained or managed him. World Famous told Whisler that he judges fights the way he sees them, that friendships don't matter once the bell rings. "I have no doubt Elizondo did just that," Whisler wrote. "And for that matter, I'm sure Townsend did the same."

Eventually the brouhaha receded and life for all the principals got back on track. The controversy never even crossed Anissa's mind a couple of months later when Lord presented her with the championship belt at a boxing event at the Austin Civic Center. Fans who had followed her career for years stood and applauded as she held the belt above her head. Outside, it was damp, cold, and miserable, and sleet pecked at the windows of the Civic Center. But Anissa never felt warmer or happier.

For her, it was a great night.

CHAPTER TWO

*Like almost all Hispanic women of that time and place,
my mother was raised to believe her role in life was to have
babies and make tortillas. And above all follow her husband's
orders. My mother was really young when she married; I
think she was still in her late teens. She never really had the
chance to find out who she was or what she wanted out of
life before she became a wife and mother. It was that babies-
and-tortillas syndrome. Don't get me wrong. There's nothing
wrong with devoting your life to that, if it's what you want
to do. I mean, if that's something you want to do, if you enjoy
that, if you want to do it, then more power to you. But a lot
of women don't want to live that kind of life. They need to
know there are other options. You can do other things. But
many women, especially Hispanic women in places away
from cities, don't think they have any choices.*

— ANISSA

. . . . .

In many ways, Anissa is the least likely of women to become a
prizefighter. Friends and family who knew her as a child would
have been hard-pressed to have predicted it. If many boxers are
first- or second-generation Americans, Anissa came from a family
with deep roots in the place where she was born and grew up. If
many boxers are molded by the sting of poverty, Anissa escaped it
as a youth—not that she knew great affluence, but she also did not
come of age on welfare.

In other ways, though, Anissa did possess qualities in common with the typical boxer. She enjoyed a natural kind of physical

grace, so picking up the nuances of the sport came fairly easy for her. She had a troubled childhood that left her with something roiling inside her that demanded to get out, and this allowed her to develop the emotional wherewithal to be able to pursue and subdue an opponent: "When the bell rings," she says, "it's just like a cockfight. You have to have that in you, that ability to go at it like those two roosters fighting each other. You have to become an animal during the fight. It's a hard-ass thing to say, but that's how it is."

Anissa was born October 24, 1970, in West Texas, far from the urban boxing venues that came to dominate her adult life. She was the third of three children. She drew her first breath in San Angelo, seat of Tom Green County, which is either a large town or small city, depending on your perspective. In a part of Texas where the vistas can be overwhelming and the population is sparse, San Angelo is a haven for health care, shopping, education, and jobs.

From its earliest days, it has had a substantial Mexican American population. In fact, Spanish padres in the community worked at converting Native Americans to Catholicism for more than two hundred years before white Texans "established" the city. Many Hispanic families in the area—such as Anissa's—have been firmly rooted there for generations. Anissa's father is a San Angelo native. Her mother comes from nearby Ballinger. Not surprisingly, the city has at times suffered through racial strife between white Texans and Hispanics, and Hispanics often found limitations on their opportunity to improve their lives. But by the time Anissa was born in San Angelo, things were changing. While members of her grandparents' generation usually could find only dead-end employment in agriculture or manual labor jobs, her parents had made the leap into the middle class. Her father sold insurance, while her mother worked at Ethicon Inc., a Johnson & Johnson subsidiary that manufactured surgical sutures and other wound-closing products.

Anissa describes the Zamarrons as an upright family living out the American dream. She spent those early years in a comfortable house in a good neighborhood. She remembers that the house was kept immaculately clean; Anissa and her brothers were allowed to play with other children only after completing their daily chores designed to keep the house spic-and-span. Her father tended to the yard on a riding lawnmower while wearing slacks, never jeans. The children attended Catholic rather than public schools. And the family regularly attended Mass. While her parents were bilingual, they refrained from speaking Spanish in the home because they wanted their children to grow up as English speakers. (Her parents had started school as Spanish-only speakers and had to learn English as they struggled to keep up with their Anglo classmates. They thought this put them at an academic disadvantage, so they wanted to ensure their own children spoke English from the get-go.) Anissa's childhood was so all-American that she even had a Mrs. Beasley doll, just like Buffy on *Family Affair*.

Her two brothers, Ramon and Roland, were, respectively, five and six years older than she. The boys were inseparable companions and Anissa idolized them, relishing moments when they would turn their attention to their tagalong little sister, even when it involved teasing her or making her the butt of a practical joke. The boys also would look out for their sister, sometimes even taking the blame for things she did wrong.

Says Anissa, "I actually do have some more or less normal childhood memories to go along with the terrible ones to come. The good ones involved Roland and Ramon when we lived in San Angelo. I have to say I was the epitome of a pesky little sister, but I craved hanging out with them, be friends. The problem was, I was only a little kid, five years old when they were ten and eleven. I had a hard time understanding why they didn't want to hang out with me. When they did let me hang with them, there was always some sort of catch. You have no idea how many times my little doll took off to the friendly skies tied to one of their kites. That's what came with getting to hang out with them. They also had ways of tricking me to stick my tongue on the end of a nine-volt battery. I fell for it a lot. You know, they'd say something about how this battery tasted different from other batteries. They'd convince me to check it out. And I'd get zapped. I can tell you right now all nine-volt batteries taste the same!"

Pranks involving nine-volt batteries aside, Roland, especially, took an interest in his little sister's well-being. Anissa came to count on him to step up for her when things weren't going her way. As a result, a particularly tight bond developed between them that persisted throughout her boxing career and beyond.

Idyllic as her days in San Angelo seem to be in her memories, not all was good. Unbeknownst to Anissa and her brothers, her parents' marriage was slowly coming unglued. Looking back on the situation, Anissa believes one problem was that her father was significantly older than her mother and had been married once before. Like many Hispanic men of his generation, he believed the husband should be the dominant member of the family, and the social mores of West Texas at the time certainly supported that viewpoint, regardless of the ethnicity of the families involved. Her mother was still in her late teens when she married Anissa's father. She coped well enough with the expectations placed on Mexican American women at that time and in that place until she reached her thirties.

"My mother had a lot of trouble with her own father," Anissa says, "and part of the reason she married my father was to get away from her family. But my mom sort of had a crisis of some sort when she hit her thirties. She will tell you that she had been an obedient wife, which was expected of her because my father—and he will tell you this—was a very traditional Mexican. She was working full-time and coming home to take care of us kids. We were still young enough to need a lot of attention. My father expected her to do all those things that a housewife is 'supposed' to do even though she had a job outside the home. On top of that, because she married so young, my mom was a sort of thirty-something woman who was still an eighteen-year-old girl inside."

In an attempt to make a fresh start after the marriage began to falter, the family left San Angelo for Austin when Anissa was seven. At first, it looked like moving to Austin would be a good thing for the family. Anissa's father was able to continue working for the same insurance company, and he made his rounds from house to house selling policies, carrying a stick to ward off biting dogs. Her mother refrained from working for a year or so after they moved so she could devote herself to being a full-time mom. Anissa was in the first grade, and she remembers that as being the best year of her childhood. Her mother gave more of herself to Anissa than she did at any other point in her life, even serving as a homeroom mom at her elementary school. Anissa thrived on the attention.

But things changed when Anissa entered the second grade. The family's finances required her mother to find a job. High-tech giant Texas Instruments hired her to work at the facility it operated at the time in far north Austin. As her mother began full-time employment again, many of the difficulties in her parents' marriage that had begun to surface in San Angelo revealed themselves once more. Her mother forged a circle of friends among her coworkers at TI, and her job and her new buddies became a significant part of her life. She and her friends rarely passed up the opportunity to enjoy happy hours at north Austin nightspots. Eventually she decided to separate from Anissa's father, leaving Roland and Ramon to live with him. From that point onward, turmoil dominated Anissa's young life.

Anissa and her mom moved to an apartment complex off Kramer Lane in what was in the late 1970s far north Austin. At the time, apartments in the area were new, catering to recently married couples, divorcees making fresh starts, and young singles beginning their careers while sowing their wilder oats in the evening and on weekends. Anissa remembers this particular complex as being for adults only, yet her mother convinced the management to let her live there with her young daughter. In retrospect, it seems it would have been better if the manager had turned down her mom's request. Anissa, just a second grader, received harsh exposure to some of the ugliest aspects of adult life while living there with her mother. "There was a lot of really rough stuff at that apartment complex," Anissa says, "stuff someone as young as

I should never have seen. Scary stuff. Really scary stuff. I grew up way too fast. I saw everything."

Not long after they moved in, a scream brought Anissa and her mother to the door of the apartment one night. They found a woman outside trying to crawl up the stairway to their apartment while shouting, "Help me! Help me!" At the same time, her boyfriend was on top of her, beating her. Anissa's mother shouted to him to leave the woman alone.

"Close that door, you fucking bitch!" the man responded. Anissa was terrified that the man would come up the stairs and attack her mother. But her mom slammed the door and called the police. At the same time, a couple of guys who shared the apartment below stepped in and started whaling on the boyfriend to make him stop slugging the woman.

Anissa went to bed that night terrified. But as time went on, it seemed as if something unsettling occurred every night. One time word spread through the complex that a rapist had been preying on women in the neighborhood. Sure enough, in the cover of night, the rapist grabbed the girlfriend of a man who lived in the apartments. Fortunately, she managed to escape and screamed for help. From the sanctuary of the apartment, Anissa could hear a great commotion coming from outside. A man from work whom her mother had begun dating, Warren,* happened to be at the apartment when the ruckus began. He hurried outside to find an angry mob running down the rapist. People were shouting, "We're gonna kill him! We're gonna fucking kill him!" Warren returned to the apartment and told Anissa's mom, "Don't you fucking open this door for anything, no matter what you hear outside." Then he rushed back outside to join the pursuit of the rapist. And, sure enough, her mother kept the door bolted tightly, a traumatized Anissa at her side.

Upsetting as the actions of the neighbors were, even more

---

* Warren is not the real name of the boyfriend. Several names have been changed in this book. A changed name, when used the first time, is designated by an asterisk.

frightening for Anissa was witnessing the mayhem within her family. The split between her mother and her father was far from amicable. Instead, angry outbursts won out, often fueled by injured pride. Anissa came to dread the distinctive *clomp-clomp-clomp* of her father's cowboy boots on the steps outside the apartment. She knew an argument between her parents likely would ensue once he arrived. As is typical with parents in the early throes of divorce, disputes often looped in the children as well, and Anissa particularly hated it when she and her brothers got involved.

Warren himself became an issue. He was a young Anglo, younger even than Anissa's mother, and her father seemed particularly upset that her mother had begun a relationship with him so quickly. For her part, Anissa despised Warren. From her perspective as a child, it was easy enough for her to blame him at least in part for the split between her parents. She also saw him as the obstacle to any chance at reconciliation.

"All this just killed me," Anissa says. "Of course I loved my mom and dad, and I was too little to really understand why there was so much anger. I really loved my brothers and I wanted to spend time with them, just like we did when we lived together. Having fun with my brothers is one of the brightest memories I have of my childhood. But everyone was so mad at everyone else, I began to wonder if they all hated me too."

One time her brothers made a point of telling her she was in no way responsible for any of the havoc besetting the family. It was a nice effort on the part of Roland and Ramon, but Anissa still harbored fears that she was somehow responsible for all that had gone wrong. It was at this time that Anissa first had inklings that something inside herself loathed her. She was far too young to understand what it was. She just knew that at times she hated herself. In years to follow, this *something* would become more fully realized in her mind, even taking on physical characteristics. She would come to consider it a demon, a particularly vicious one that was fiercely angry at everything and everybody—especially at herself. But for now it manifested itself as a self-loathing that left her perplexed and frightened.

With all the chaos brought about by the fracturing family and with her parents' time commitments of jobs and new romantic relationships, Anissa began to feel emotionally neglected by the adults surrounding her. In fact, it sometimes seemed to her as if she didn't even exist to them. Anissa especially craved much more attention from her mother, yearning for the kind of relationship she had had with her during that first year in Austin. But her mother began working nights and devoting her free time to partying with Warren and her buddies from work—by this time, her mother had switched jobs, moving from Texas Instruments to the large IBM facility off Burnet Road in Austin, where she'd be employed for the remainder of Anissa's school years. There just weren't enough hours in the day for work and play and for Anissa. Anissa believed she lost out.

Her mother had a difficult time finding dependable child-care services for Anissa, so Anissa felt as if she was shifted from stranger to stranger. One day the revolving door of babysitters stopped at an elderly woman's house. The woman was to watch Anissa through the night, then walk her to her school, Wooldridge Elementary, the next morning. But the next morning, the old woman didn't get up. Anissa went to her bedroom and found that the woman had become very ill during the night.

"I'm sorry," the woman told her, "but I'm too sick to walk you to school. You'll have to go by yourself."

Anissa was truly alarmed by her words. This was a strange house in a strange neighborhood, and she knew it was a long way from her school. But Anissa also could tell from the way the old woman looked and sounded that she was not lying: She was indeed quite sick. So Anissa screwed up her courage and set out the front door, determined to make it to school by herself—and she got lost. But she didn't give up. She kept walking until she found a familiar street, Peyton Gin Road, and figured out how to get to Wooldridge. As she trudged along, near Lanier High School, she passed two older boys going the other direction.

"Hey, it's 'Nissa!" she heard. She turned around and saw that the two boys she'd passed were Roland and Ramon. "Aren't you going to speak to your brothers? How ya doing?"

"I'm good. How are you guys?"

"We're good."

Then they went on their way.

Years later, Anissa would reflect on that encounter frequently. Not too long before that, she and her brothers were part of a tight family unit. Now they seemed like acquaintances she hadn't seen in a long time—not family members, just "regular people" you'd run into on the street. When she and Roland talk about those days now, Roland always tells her that he felt sorry for her because he had Ramon, someone he could bond with during that particularly trying time. Separated from her brothers, Anissa had no one. By the time Anissa was in the third grade, she sometimes felt as if she were on her own.

As an adult, Anissa sat down one afternoon and came up with this assessment of her relationship with her family and the other adults surrounding her during her childhood and adolescence: "As I've looked back over the years, I've realized that people were just doing the best they could at the time, given the circumstances they faced and the tools they had to use. You know what I mean? Besides, I've had a lot of experience in my life being around bitter people who carried a lot of rage and resentment with them. I never saw them happy. And I sure as hell don't want to be like them. What's happened has happened and can't be changed. I'd rather get on with living as good a life as I can live."

At the time, though, living that good life seemed entirely out of her reach.

. . . . .

As often happens with children who feel emotionally neglected, Anissa learned she could get attention if she misbehaved. Few rewards came for doing well in school and otherwise "being good," but "being bad" made people around her aware of her existence.

Even though harsh punishment generally came with that awareness, it was better than feeling ignored.

Anissa began to let her angry impulses manifest themselves in violent acts. For the remainder of her elementary school years and continuing through her adolescence, these episodes brought further havoc into Anissa's life. The scariest part for her was that she never knew when the impulse would strike.

She has a vivid memory of the first time it happened. Her mother went shopping, leaving Warren and Anissa alone at the apartment. Anissa had gone outside to play while Warren was doing some housekeeping. Suddenly, Anissa stopped playing as rage overtook her. As if in a trance, she walked back to the apartment building, climbed the stairs, and stomped in the front door. She found Warren in the bathroom scrubbing the tub. He was bent over with his back toward Anissa. Without giving him any sort of warning, Anissa quickly rushed toward him and shoved him, sending him sprawling into the tub. "It was almost like something from a scary movie," she recalls. "You know, where a little kid is just playing like normal but suddenly picks up a big butcher knife and starts stabbing people. It wasn't like I thought about it before I did it. It just happened." The fall into the bathtub left Warren with an injured shoulder.

Anissa's behavior troubled her mother and the other people around her, none of whom were really sure what they were witnessing. Most of the time, Anissa was a sweet little girl with a big, winning smile and a tomboy bent. But then there would be those dark episodes that seemed to come out of nowhere. What did all this mean? Was something seriously wrong with her? Or was she just an undisciplined brat at times?

Her mother struggled with this more than anyone. As time went on, the relationship between mother and daughter grew complicated. Anissa had a lot of admiration for her mother. "She was drop-dead gorgeous, for one thing," Anissa says. "I mean, my mother was hot. She left my father for a guy who was a twenty-something, you know, a big age difference. That tells you a lot." But what Anissa really admired was her mother's strength. If the West Texas standard for Hispanic women was that they be demure and deferential to the men in their lives, Anissa's mom smashed the mold. "She was tough. I guess that's the main reason I looked up to her. You just didn't fuck with her, you know? If you did, she'd chew you up and spit you out like you were nothing. She was a strong, independent woman who pretty much went down the road she wanted to travel once she divorced my father. I wanted to be a strong woman like she was. I wanted people to respect me the way they would her. I wanted to be tough like her, I wanted to be pretty like her."

On the other hand, Anissa found herself growing frustrated by her mother's inability to understand when Anissa was emotionally out of kilter. Part of the problem was that between the demands of work and her desire for a social life, her mother didn't witness firsthand many of the incidents when Anissa turned into a "demon child." While she found Warren's presence upsetting, Anissa tended to behave well when she was at home with just her mother or her brothers there for company. More and more, her worst behavior came out at school. When school officials reported discipline problems back to her mother, what they described was far out of character for the Anissa she knew at home. "She couldn't buy it was happening," Anissa says. "When she'd go up to the school, she went with her mind set that she wasn't going to buy any of their shit. She was going to defend her daughter, and that meant she was going to give them hell. She'd think that the damned school was trying to fuck me over, and she wasn't about to put up with that. She just couldn't see the same kid the school authorities saw. But then, when everything really surfaced and she realized just how bad I was at school—well, she just got really confused. That Anissa turned out to be so different from what she thought I was. She just didn't know what to do."

One night her mother came into Anissa's bedroom and said, "What's wrong with you?"

That particular night, Anissa, though still a child, was obsessed with just one thought—she wanted to die. She looked up at her mother, but she couldn't find a way to make the words come out—how does someone tell anyone that, especially her mother?

So Anissa said nothing. Says Anissa, "I remember wanting to tell her. She even said to me that she knew it was on the tip of my tongue. But I knew better than to say anything. I don't know what she would have done if I had told her. I had this vision of her getting angry, dragging me through the house to the medicine cabinet and showing me some pills and saying, 'You want to kill yourself? Here, take these!' Or saying, 'Here's a gun, do it!' It was a crazy vision, of course. My mom wouldn't have done that. But that's not how I saw things at the time. So I just played it safe and kept my mouth shut."

Anissa believes her mother was confused, frustrated, and desperate. She tried everything to get Anissa back on track, including tactics that maybe weren't the best thought out. "One thing she did was constantly ridicule me," Anissa says. "I get angry even today when I think back to how she'd make fun of me. Like those times I was trying to read out loud. This was when I was still in grade school. I read real slow, and she'd laugh at me, get my brothers to laugh at me too. They'd ride me something terrible, and I'd get so mad at them I'd think I was going to blow up.

"Roland helped me though. You see, sometimes I'd have a lot of trouble with schoolwork. Some other times, I'd do real good, get on the honor roll and stuff like that. But I went through a difficult period trying to learn how to add and subtract. Mom, she wouldn't show me how at all. One night, I couldn't do my arithmetic homework because I didn't understand adding and subtracting. When I asked Mom for help, she yelled at me until I started crying. Then she just left, went to get the laundry or something. I was real upset, didn't know what I was going to do. Then Roland came up to me and said, 'Hey, 'Nissa, look, it's really easy. Let me show you.' He just calmly explained how it worked and that's how I learned adding and subtracting, thanks to my brother just jumping in."

· · · · ·

Anissa and her mother moved from the apartment in north Austin to a house in the rapidly growing suburb of Round Rock. She remembers the house as being located in what at the time was a nice, stable middle-class neighborhood just off Sam Bass Road. But things at home were anything but nice and stable. Roland and Ramon had not gotten along with their father, and things got worse when their father began a relationship with the woman who eventually began living at his house. The boys wound up moving in with their mother and sister and enrolled at Round Rock High School. With their mother gone so much of the time working at IBM, her brothers had plenty of opportunity to cut up when the kids had the house to themselves, sometimes carrying on until all hours of the morning. When this happened, Anissa found it difficult to sleep, so she'd arrive at school in the morning already feeling exhausted. She began nodding off during class. It happened often enough to alarm school officials, who notified her mother about the problem. They also arranged for her to have sessions with a school counselor to try to resolve the issue. Anissa herself came up with at least a partial solution: She started going to sleep at night in the clothes she'd wear to school the next day. That way, she could sleep until the last minute before jumping out of bed to head to the classroom.

Anissa also wasn't eating well. Because her mother worked evenings, she expected the older boys to ensure their little sister had dinner. But both Roland and Ramon got fast-food jobs, which required them to be at work immediately after school and kept them busy until midnight. Anissa sometimes found herself alone in the house in the evening with nothing to eat. "Everybody tried so hard," she says. "But it was just how the cards fell. Mom was working odd shifts, you know, trying to make a little extra money to have a nice house for her kids. With teenage boys in the house, the food she bought quickly disappeared. Some days there just wasn't any food in the house. This is hard to say, but there were mornings when I had to scrounge through the trash to find something to eat, maybe some old pizza crusts or something."

And, complicating everything else, Anissa entered puberty very early. In the fifth grade, she began to develop breasts. None of the other girls in her class were doing that yet, and she felt ashamed of it. She dreaded being the first girl in her class to wear a bra, fearing it would call attention to herself—she envisioned fifth-grade boys sneaking up to pop the straps—in a humiliating way. She didn't feel like she was getting much help at home in dealing with the situation: Her mother's boyfriend at the time, Warren, would tease her about sprouting "nasty brown things." His teasing, coming from a white man she disliked, was difficult to take. Anissa reacted by trying to hide the changes her body was going through. She began wearing a loose-fitting navy blue hoodie that covered her up. She wore it almost constantly. Even in hot weather, the hoodie stayed on. Her refusal to remove it eventually got her sent to the principal's office. With the constant wear, it had grown filthy.

"At that time," Anissa says, "I was just wild-looking anyway. I was pretty much a ratty thing in a nasty, snotty, dirty hoodie who didn't even know how to try to fix her hair. I remember once when I did run a comb through my hair, and everybody was like, Anissa! You combed your hair!"

. . . . .

Not all was dismal for her during elementary school. In the fifth grade, she got her first real exposure to athletics and loved what she experienced. The grubby hoodie hid not only a budding adolescent but also a potential athlete. Years later, she would wonder what difference it might have made in her life if she had been able to develop as an athlete at an earlier age.

"This guy who was a PE teacher used to just annoy the hell out of me the year before, when I was in the fourth grade," Anissa says. "You know, I wasn't like the top performer at anything in PE and if I didn't do as well as I could have at something, he would say stuff to me like, 'Get up off your pity pot!' That used to really piss me off. But things changed in the fifth grade. One day the class went down to Town Lake in Austin for a demonstration of Frisbee football, and we all got to play some. When we came back to Round Rock, this PE teacher who used to annoy me so much said to me, 'You know, you have a lot of athletic ability.' That made me feel just incredible. No one had ever told me that I had ability at anything before. You know, I was like most kids. I wanted to be part of sports, maybe a member of a team of some sort. But with everyone working and so busy with everything, no one had time to take me to practices, then pick me up afterward. So I never got to participate."

She was able to join a running club at her elementary school, however. The club trained during the lunch hour, so no one needed to take her to practices or pick her up afterward. She received direct rewards for participating in races—T-shirts and medals. But beyond that, it developed in her a love of running for running's sake. It would lay dormant for many years, but when she began boxing training in earnest when she was in her early twenties, that love of running resurfaced, much to her benefit.

. . . . .

As Anissa moved from elementary school to middle school, all the self-encouragement she'd received from participating in Frisbee football and the running club evaporated. Her sixth-grade classes seemed to be much more challenging than her fifth-grade classes had been, and she floundered trying to keep up. She was now surrounded by older kids, and the pressures of adolescence grew more intense. Topping all that, her parents' divorce became final. By this time, her mother and father had been apart for several years, and it was apparent to everyone familiar with the situation that they would never reconcile. Still, something about the formality of the actual divorce sent Anissa over the edge. She stopped caring about just about everything. "I can see myself going in to take a final exam in school, and you know what? I don't even write my name on the paper. I think you got a few points just for writing your name on the test. But I didn't want any points. I just left it blank."

As if her life wasn't in turmoil enough, it was in the sixth grade that she began to find stashes of marijuana and alcohol. She liked what she found and started getting stoned and drunk whenever she had the chance. On top of that, she experimented with amphetamines—in particular the prescription capsules known on the street as black mollies—again thanks to a hidden stash she happened upon.

IBM transferred her mother's boyfriend, Warren, to New York, and shortly after that, her mother broke off the relationship. Now without a boyfriend, she began dating around, which upped the amount of time she devoted to her social life. Sometimes she'd travel with her friends, leaving Anissa's teenage brothers in charge of the house. Not surprisingly, the boys used this as an opportunity to ratchet up their own partying. Anissa, though significantly younger, became part of that party scene, hanging out with high school kids: "Not long ago I ran into the guy who was like the oldest kid in that bunch. He told me, 'Wow, Anissa, you were like the coolest twelve-year-old ever!' Of course, that's what I wanted people to think. I figured my brothers didn't want a little kid hanging out with them. So I just stopped being a little kid. I got to know these guys who played in a rock 'n' roll band, and they'd get me stoned and drunk and everyone thought it was just so cool. Not only that, the kids in my class began to think I was the shit because I was hanging with high school kids. So I was getting some recognition, which I always craved, but I was getting recognized for all the wrong reasons."

Her rage-fired outbursts at school became more frequent and more intense, no doubt adding to the bad-ass reputation she enjoyed. She would pitch fits in classes or start slamming her fists into lockers, which would get her into hot water with school officials. Or she'd become withdrawn and quiet, her surly glare challenging someone to ask her if something was wrong. Her teachers began to suspect something was seriously amiss with her, something that far exceeded typical teenage moodiness.

But her teachers and even her family at this point had no concept of the depth of her problems. The worst revealed itself when she was alone. Everything around her seemed out of control. But she discovered there was one thing over which she could have power. And so one day she slugged herself in the face to make her nose bleed. The sight of her blood sent a thrill through her. So she began hitting herself in private to achieve the prize of making her blood flow. Eventually she began to use a razor to slice her skin open—now that was something she could control, whether or not to cut herself, whether or not to punish herself with sharp steel. The idea seemed to come out of nowhere. She knew of no one else doing it, had not even heard of anyone doing it. But from the very first it gave her satisfaction in a way nothing else could. It was punishment, yes, and she felt an overwhelming need to punish herself, but she also got a high from doing it. As soon as she saw her own blood, she felt a rush that even amphetamines or a line of blow couldn't top. As her experimentation with cutting continued, she discovered that the more often she did it, the bigger the rush she would receive.

Of course, those highs from cutting came at an extreme cost, beyond even the physical damage she inflicted on herself. Anissa felt enormous shame because of it, felt like a freak, certain she was the only person in the world who could do such a hideous thing. She had no way of knowing she was not alone. In fact, other kids at her middle school were no doubt doing the same thing and suffering the same solitary guilt pangs as Anissa—cutting is practiced by hundreds of thousands, if not millions, of troubled Americans, most of them adolescent girls, virtually all of whom are grappling with the need to control emotional pain. Psychologist Wendy Lader says cutters tend to "have a history of sexual, physical, or verbal abuse. Most are sensitive, perfectionists, overachievers. The self-injury begins as a defense against what's going on in their family, in their lives. They have failed in one area of their lives, so this is a way to get control." Everyone who takes it up discovers the same hard lesson that Anissa learned: Once you start cutting, it becomes compulsive. Anissa continued to cut herself for more than five years.

Back at school, at this time still unaware of Anissa's bloody private escapades, her teachers decided she suffered symptoms of attention deficit disorder, or as it's more commonly called today, attention deficit/hyperactivity disorder (ADHD). They encouraged her to find activities into which she could invest her surplus energy. One thing Anissa tried was music.

Like many kids, Anissa had fantasies of becoming a rock star; Anissa particularly idolized Pat Benatar, and she dreamed of standing in the spotlight, just like Benatar, receiving a thunderous ovation from thousands of adoring fans. Her family was musical. Her father played Mexican American border music on a classical guitar and her brothers took piano lessons. After Anissa expressed an interest in performing, her father bought her a classical guitar and enrolled her in lessons. While this instilled a lifelong love of guitar, Anissa found the lessons frustrating. The process of learning was taking too long to allow her to make it an outlet for her surplus energy. Besides, neither classical nor Tex-Mex music could fire up her soul. She wanted to rock. Whenever her guitar instructor would leave the room, Anissa took the opportunity to show her fellow students a riff or two from Ozzy Osbourne's metal classic "Crazy Train" or some other heavy tune far removed from the typical fare played on a gut-string acoustical guitar.

Her guitar instructor recommended that she transfer to rock lessons. In the years to come, her interest in guitar playing would rise, then ebb—today she plays a black Fender Stratocaster, although her preferences are more toward blues-based music than toward Ozzy—but it never became more than a hobby. Her need for *something* to be on the receiving end of her passion and her raw energy went unfulfilled. She wouldn't know the thrill of the ovation until many years later, and then it came by way of boxing, not music.

. . . . .

Her problems at school worsened to the extent that teachers gave her their home phone numbers with instructions for her to call them if she ever needed help. She also came to the attention of a juvenile officer with the Round Rock Police Department, Mike

Oates.* In Oates, Anissa found someone who was willing to listen when she wanted to discuss her problems. He understood her family situation and empathized with the problems she battled. "That was a big deal," Anissa says, "having an adult in a position of authority who cared about me. He had a daughter about my age, so I guess he could relate firsthand to a lot I was going through. He was able to help me a lot." But Anissa also discovered that Oates would allow himself to be manipulated by her. She disliked her fourth-period class and there were days when she just didn't want to attend it. So she would telephone Oates and say, "Hey, Mike, I *really* need to talk. Why don't you come get me out of fourth period?" She knew that if a juvenile officer came to school and requested to see her, the school would excuse her from class. To be sure, Anissa found the discussions that followed with Oates to be helpful. But still, her underlying motivation to see him often was rooted in a desire to cut class.

A teacher at the middle school, Helen Corry,* spent extra time trying to help Anissa. But in spite of the best efforts of people like Oates and Corry, Anissa eventually got it in her mind that she wasn't worthy of anything. One day she had been sent home from school for misbehaving. Knowing what would happen when her mother came home from work, she sliced her wrists. She telephoned Corry and told her she was contemplating suicide, although she didn't tell her that she'd already lacerated herself. Within moments, three police cars arrived at her house. "Now, we didn't live in the slums or anything," Anissa says. "We were living in a nice house in a good neighborhood, and seeing a bunch of cop cars roaring in wasn't something the neighbors were used to seeing. For some reason, I'd covered up my wrists, so the cops never saw that I had actually already cut them. If they had, I would have been shipped off to an institution right away." And remarkably that's how it ended, with no one any the wiser about her self-mutilation.

The next academic year turned out to be even worse. School officials labeled her "emotionally disturbed" and put her into special education classes in the alternative learning center. While the stigma of special ed may have been difficult to swallow, she did have access for the first time to a psychologist. But that didn't seem to help much.

Finally there came a day when Anissa let the whole world know just how seriously disturbed she was:

> I had gotten in trouble in class, probably for being disruptive or something. I went into the assistant principal's office and sat down with my bad self. By this time, the school and my mom were getting pretty fed up with me. The assistant principal said he was going to have to call my mom to have her come and pick me up. I knew that if that happened, she'd go off on me somehow. I begged him not to do it. I said I'd straighten up. But he went ahead and started dialing a number on the telephone. I freaked when he did that and started punching myself in the nose. I mean, I hit myself a lot and blood started flowing. I'm talking about a bunch of blood. I knew from what I'd been doing to myself in private that the nose is a good place to draw blood, but I'd never done anything like this in public before. Everybody freaked. My mom was called. My juvie officer was called. My secret was out. I can remember just sitting there in this Journey concert T-shirt covered in blood. The juvie officer, Mike Oates, shows up and said to me that he was surprised, that he thought my mother and I were doing better. I was totally embarrassed. I didn't say anything. I had nothing to say. It was all out there in the open now. There was no hiding the blood all over my Journey shirt. When my mom got there, they told us Child Protective Services had been called as well and that they would be contacting us. I wasn't to return to school until I had a psychological evaluation. The ride home was pretty quiet. The only thing I remember my mother saying was "You're fucking nuts," and then she shook her head. It sounds kind of cold-blooded, but that was her way. I think she was just scared. I think she finally began to realize just how bad off I was.

After meeting with Anissa and her mom, a CPS counselor determined that Anissa fit the pattern of a habitual cutter, and that she was suicidal. In short, very much a danger to herself. The counselor contacted a private practice psychologist, Dr. Joan Laughlin,* and recommended Anissa begin therapy with her. After her mom cleared it with her health insurance, Anissa began seeing Dr. Laughlin. When Anissa had mentioned suicidal thoughts to her family earlier, they tended to dismiss it as the words of a typical teenage drama queen, complete overstatement in an attempt to get attention. Believing that giving in to such drama would be the wrong thing to do, they reacted scornfully in most cases, often taunting her. But now everyone knew the depths of Anissa's problems, and all involved hoped Dr. Laughlin could provide a remedy.

If she had been frightened about what lay ahead earlier, Anissa actually felt a sense of relief on the day she first entered Dr. Laughlin's office. After inviting Anissa to have a seat, Dr. Laughlin looked at her and said, "Anissa, do you believe you need help?"

There was no hesitation. "Yes, I do. I know what I'm doing is wrong."

Dr. Laughlin smiled and nodded. "Well, we're going to get you some help." Two days later, Anissa entered a mental hospital for the first time.

CHAPTER THREE

*Rush is the term used in psychiatric health facilities when
the staff has to react to a patient who's gone fucking out of
control. I almost got addicted to being rushed, you know?
It was a way of getting attention, and it was a kind of
release because I got my energy out. But the big thing was
it involved touching, which I know sounds kind of weird.
But you have to remember, my mom never hugged me or
anything, it was unthinkable to even ask for a hug, and I
craved the human touch, just like any person would.*

— ANISSA

. . . . .

Shoal Creek Hospital takes its name from a flood-prone stream
nearby that flows through central Austin, roughly parallel to
MoPac Expressway. The facility is situated on the western edge
of a neighborhood dominated by hospitals, clinics, and medical
supply businesses close to the intersection of Lamar Boulevard
and Thirty-fourth Street. From the outside, Shoal Creek Hospital
looks rather unexceptional. An uninformed passerby would never
guess that the building houses patients engaged in the worst kinds
of battles against mental illness, substance abuse, or both.

On the Saturday following the cutting incident in the assistant
principal's office, Anissa and her mother drove from their house in
Round Rock to Shoal Creek. They were both crying. Even though
Anissa was still a child, she shared with her mother an understanding of the gravity of what was about to happen. This was
very serious business. But Anissa agreed with her mom that she
could not go on behaving in the way she had been: Something had

to change. Her mother believed she was out of options, that the bloody incident at middle school was the final straw. Anissa could not argue with that.

After arriving, Anissa and her mother sat through the tedious procedure that's fairly standard for admission to any sort of hospital, which Anissa remembers as being centered around the all-important insurance card. One good thing about Shoal Creek was that Anissa would be allowed to wear her street clothes; she wouldn't be stuck in the sort of scrubs or pajamas seen on patients in movies like *One Flew Over the Cuckoo's Nest.* So Anissa had a suitcase with her, filled with her everyday attire. Once all the paperwork had been completed, Anissa, clutching the suitcase, followed a staff member upstairs to the juvenile unit and the room she would be calling home for the next few months. She was introduced to the few people present in the unit—because it was a weekend, many staffers had the day off and many patients were absent on weekend passes.

The unit itself was a corridor of patient rooms, with a nurses' station at one end and a dayroom at the other, all behind locked doors. The patient rooms were similar to what you'd find in a college dorm—small, functional, with a couple of beds, a dresser, a bathroom. Private televisions and telephones were prohibited. Patients could watch the solitary TV in the dayroom, which also had a pay phone. During Anissa's first day on the floor, no one showed her the area beyond the nurses' station. Soon enough, however, she'd learn that this was where the psychiatric intensive care unit (PICU) was housed.

As Anissa settled in at Shoal Creek, she battled conflicting emotions. She'd never been separated from her mother before, so she felt frightened and homesick as soon as her mother left her at the hospital. At the same time, she hoped that being away from home and all the psychological baggage she associated with her mother's house would help her start feeling better about herself. In the end, the fear and homesickness won out. As a new patient, Anissa was placed under observation by the hospital staff, and she could not leave the corridor of patient rooms. "I hated it," she says, "and I cried and cried and cried. 'I don't belong here!' I'd tell people. 'I'm not like these other kids!' Meaning that I was not crazy like them.

"It's hard to describe what goes on inside your head when you're messed up like I was. In those early days, Dr. Laughlin would take me outside sometimes and everything was great. She thought I was a sweet little kid, a nice little girl who was so cooperative and who was so up for getting better. But when I went back inside the unit, something inside of me switched. I managed to stay pretty quiet for the first week. But then I started exploding, I started becoming this hellion. Hey, it was okay to throw chairs or do anything else I wanted to do. 'Fuck it!' was my attitude. I'd just go nuts.

"That's how I came to learn about being rushed."

It happened soon after her arrival at Shoal Creek. She was shouting and threw a chair. Suddenly she found herself enveloped by hospital staffers. A gurney arrived. The techs and nurses put her on the gurney and held her in place with their bodies while someone strapped her down. Once they secured her on the gurney, they rushed her out of the corridor and into the PICU, where they took her off the gurney and locked her in a seclusion room. She quickly learned she'd be confined to this room until she settled down. "If you'd stay quiet for thirty minutes," Anissa says, "they'd crack the door as a reward. I started to figure out that everything was going to be built around this kind of reward-and-punishment system. If you stayed calm for another thirty minutes, they'd take you back to the unit. That's what you wanted. But, even if you were calm, they wouldn't let you go back to the unit if they thought you were a threat to cause more trouble. If they thought that, they'd actually transfer you from the juvenile unit to PICU. And you didn't want that."

Anissa learned she'd have her own room in PICU if and when she was transferred there. She'd be segregated from the other kids in the juvenile unit and she didn't want that. For instance, she'd have to eat in solitude back there while the other patients dined together. She'd be on complete restriction and have to earn all privileges. To be able to watch TV for thirty minutes, she'd first have to write a paper with a topic like "How I Can Control My Anger." Everything was rigid and controlled, and Anissa would hate her time in PICU.

And yet she found herself intentionally doing things to get rushed in order to receive attention. The situation confused her. She fought the techs and nurses throughout the process, yet she wanted what was happening to her. She believed her resistance was essential because it masked her true motivation for causing trouble in the first place. If she'd placidly gone along with rushes, it would have been transparent to the staff that what she really sought was attention. If the nurses and techs realized that, undoubtedly they would have reacted differently. The fighting also made it easier for Anissa herself to accept her behavior. She wanted everyone at Shoal Creek to respect her as a bad-ass rather than dismiss her as some pathetic little girl who caused trouble because she craved attention.

But when Dr. Laughlin came around, Anissa adopted an entirely different persona. Anissa became a sweet little kid, a nice girl who was dedicated to doing whatever it took to get well. Dr. Laughlin sometimes conducted their sessions outdoors, where Anissa felt freed from all the turmoil she associated with being on the unit. But then Dr. Laughlin would leave, Anissa would return to the confines of the unit, and her dark side would reemerge.

There were times when a rush procedure wasn't adequate to get her under control. Those episodes prompted the nurses to begin giving her injections of Thorazine to calm her. The nurses also encouraged her to begin requesting the drug whenever she felt edgy. They provided it to her in pill form in those cases so she could administer it to herself. She remembers getting carried away once with the Thorazine. The juvenile unit day was divided into two parts: Patients spent half a day in therapy, the other half in the school set up in the unit. The day she'd taken so much Thorazine, she went to the classroom, and, bang, her head abruptly fell on her desk. The teacher tried reviving her to no avail and went for assistance. The staff helped her to her room, where she spent the rest of the day sleeping off the effects of the drug.

"I know being rushed and the Thorazine injections sound bad," Anissa explains. "But the fact of the matter is that I wanted to stay at Shoal Creek once I got over being homesick during those first days. If you knew all the shit I caused there, you might have thought I hated it. But there were people at Shoal Creek who cared about me, who wanted me to get better, to be happy. I'd never felt that before. One thing that was bad about my home life was that I never felt safe in my own house. But at Shoal Creek, I felt secure. So, yes, I was causing all these problems but it also was the place I wanted to be."

Anissa's relationship with the other patients at times could be difficult—"a lot of them thought I was a pain in the ass." Her first roommate was a girl whose parents had her admitted to Shoal Creek after she made a halfhearted attempt at suicide. The first time she witnessed Anissa entering into one of her rages, the girl was frightened and wanted a different roommate. When word of what happened spread to the other kids, none wanted to share a room with Anissa. In spite of occurrences like that, when she was on an even keel, Anissa could get along well with the other patients.

She was one of the youngest patients in the unit. Moreover, she was from what a lot of people consider the drab suburb of Round Rock, while many of the kids were from hip neighborhoods in Austin. Because of this, she didn't feel nearly as sophisticated as the others. She'd listen admiringly as they described their high jinks on the Drag, a section of Guadalupe Street adjacent to the University of Texas. Over endless games of spades in the dayroom, these older kids took a liking to Anissa. It made her feel good to be accepted by them.

Anissa would come to express mixed opinions about Shoal Creek. At times she would say that she didn't accomplish much in the way of seriously addressing her core problems at the hospital. But at other times she would concede it was during her first stay at Shoal Creek that she learned one fundamental lesson that contributed to her eventual improvement: She thrived in a structured environment. "When someone puts structure into your life," she says, "it means that person cares about you. Ideally, your parents would do it because they love you. Sure, at Shoal Creek the staff did what they did because they were paid to do it. Even though they were being paid to care, they nevertheless cared. I got my needs met, I got good food, and, like I said, I felt safe. We were given responsibilities and we were expected to meet those responsibilities. If you met your responsibilities, you got a reward."

Over the years, Anissa would be diagnosed and rediagnosed as suffering from everything from schizophrenia to bipolar disorder. Finally, the doctors settled on borderline personality disorder (BPD) as the source of her problems. Anissa's was an almost textbook case of BPD. BPD symptoms usually begin to show up during childhood and involve self-destructive behavior, unstable emotions, impulsiveness, relationship problems, and an unstable self-image. Patients have difficulty controlling anger, and they often fear being abandoned. One problem health-care providers face with BPD is that no one really knows what causes it. Some experts suspect that BPD, like many psychological disorders, is caused by a brain chemistry imbalance. Environmental factors almost certainly contribute to it as well. Genetics might play a role, too.

A study published by the American Psychiatric Association shows that teens whose parents have it are five times more likely to get it themselves. It also turns up more often among children with family members who have antisocial behavior disorder, substance abuse problems, or mood disorders like depression. And women are much more likely to suffer from it than men, especially if they've gone through significant childhood trauma. BPD patients do best when they live an ordered life, with appropriate sleep, a balanced diet, plenty of exercise, positive relationships with family and friends, and the avoidance of alcohol and recreational drugs.

So the structured life she led at Shoal Creek definitely helped Anissa to feel better. But at the end of her three-month stay—the longest a short-term patient could remain at the hospital—the doctors believed she was far from well. They recommended that she be admitted for long-term care at a residential treatment center. Long-term care implies months and months, possibly years of treatment. That prospect terrified Anissa, although her mother believed it would be best for her. Her father interceded and said no.

"Anissa," he told her, "you can come live with me."

. . . . .

She lived with her father for the next six months. During her stay at Shoal Creek, she'd fallen far behind in her studies, so she trailed other students significantly when she began attending public school again. That was a source of stress. But otherwise, she remembers life at her father's house as going fairly well, at least for a while. Occasionally she was disorderly at school, but not to the degree she'd been before Shoal Creek. The impulse to cut herself went away. With her father's encouragement, she began karate lessons, which she loved.

Her father acted with good intentions when he offered to let Anissa live with him, but he was busy working and therefore absent from the house a good deal of the time. Knowing no one would be home, Anissa would stay at the karate school for as long as she could, participating in all the classes available, then head to the Stop-n-Go convenience store for a bag of chips and a Coke, which would suffice for dinner. This lack of a stable home life made her vulnerable for her illness to return. It did just that when the holiday season arrived. There was a lot of family turmoil surrounding the holidays that year, and in response to it, Anissa tried to kill herself by slashing her wrists. On the Wednesday before Christmas, she was readmitted to Shoal Creek as a short-term patient.

Anissa remembers that her second trip to Shoal Creek turned out to be much more productive than the first one. "For one thing, I made friends with the other patients, and I got to know the staff much, much better. You know, some of them really dreaded the news that I was coming back because I'd been so difficult to deal with the first time. They thought I was a big pain in the ass. To them, it was like, 'Oh no! Anissa's coming back. That's just great!'

But for whatever reason — maybe it was because I was familiar with the place — I was ready to do some work on myself. I was making levels, going on outings, doing really good. I wasn't well, not by any means, but I wasn't nearly as bad as I was the first time. I did so much better with relationships and stuff.

"I liked Shoal Creek better the second time around and accomplished some things to address my condition, but I didn't get any serious work done, you know? The work at the foundation of the problem. That's why I kept fucking up and coming back. It just didn't work for me for the long term. Maybe for some kids it did, but for me it didn't. It was fun from the fact that I liked it and I would probably want to stay there forever, but I wasn't getting anything accomplished. At Shoal Creek, it was more about the kids talking — like they would talk in depth about their relationship with their father or something. Some of the boys would talk about fathers especially. I don't know, like, maybe they didn't really have a father. Or maybe he was there physically but not there in a meaningful way. Whatever — things like that. The kids would talk about some deep stuff, you know, like when they were small as opposed to now, and do things like speculate that maybe they started drinking and smoking dope because their dad was a big partyer. And sometimes we would go from that to really deep stuff, like being sexually abused. So maybe it helped those kids, but I wasn't getting down on my issues, the heart of them, you know?"

One relationship that Anissa came to value developed outside Shoal Creek. After her romance with Warren ended, Anissa's mother married a man named Michael,* whom she'd met shortly before Anissa went to Shoal Creek the first time. While Anissa resented and otherwise disliked Warren, she had great affection for Michael. A financial analyst for IBM, Michael was a man with three grown children who showed mature judgment. Early in her mother and Michael's relationship, Anissa had gotten drunk at a Mr. Gatti's pizza restaurant and vomited "all over everything." Her mother came to get her. Once Anissa was in the car, her mother chastised her angrily. But once they got home, coolheaded Michael defused the situation, calming everyone down. Such acts of compassion made the connection between stepdaughter and stepfather a good one. "Right off the bat," she remembers, "Michael and I hit it off." Anissa's mother and Michael made an agreement: If they married, they'd stick with it for five years. Indeed, their marriage lasted five years. During that time, Michael was there for Anissa, visiting her in mental institutions as regularly as any blood relative would.

But the bond between Anissa and Michael failed to improve seriously worsening emotional problems. She fell further and further behind in school. She was back in special education classes and eventually was prescribed Ritalin to address her ADHD. Yet nothing seemed to be helping with her violent outbursts. She spent a summer anticipating her first year at Round Rock High School. But the early weeks of the school year turned out to be one of the darkest periods in her life, and her academic year ended before it really began. She was smoking a lot of marijuana at the time, especially before going to class. Between classes, she might climb a tree on campus, and when school officials ordered her to climb down, she'd reply, "Fuck you! I ain't comin' down." And she'd stay there until she was good and ready to lower herself from the branches.

Finally, a violence-tinged confrontation near a Pizza Hut across a street from the temporary buildings housing the school's special ed classes essentially ended her public school experience altogether. It began with Anissa throwing chairs in class and then threatening the life of a substitute teacher before it spilled outside. The police were called. A psychologist who had been treating Anissa attempted to arrange another stay at Shoal Creek. But the facility declined to admit her again. Besides, it was becoming clear to all involved that further short-term treatment was not likely to help her improve.

Dr. Laughlin, the psychologist who had been treating Anissa, suggested long-term treatment and attempted to gain admission for her into the Timberlawn Mental Health System. Timberlawn was and remains a well-respected organization operating both in- and outpatient facilities in the Dallas–Fort Worth metropolitan area. The plan was for Anissa to enter its acute in-patient treatment program. Unfortunately, as it turned out, Timberlawn had no vacancies. Placing Anissa on a waiting list was not a feasible option, given the dire need she had for immediate and intense care.

Dallas's Brookhaven Pavilion, run by the Psychiatric Institutes of America (PIA) subsidiary of National Medical Enterprises (NME), a California-based for-profit health-care corporation, did have a vacancy, and given the urgency of the situation, Anissa wound up there. As she entered Brookhaven, neither Anissa nor her family had any notion that Brookhaven was part of an operation designed to exploit patients and their insurance companies. In years to come, news organizations nationwide, including the *New York Times*, would report on the scandal involving Brookhaven and other PIA/NME facilities. In the end, there would be successful criminal prosecutions, tens of millions of dollars paid in fines and lawsuit settlements, testimony given to a congressional subcommittee by former patients alleging abuse, an investigation by the Texas attorney general, and hospitals ordered to close their doors as a result of their practice of illegal patient imprisonment in order to obtain health insurance payments.

At the time, though, Anissa's family could not have known she was being viewed as a "head on a bed" so her insurance company could be billed for the cost of her confinement. Daunting as the prospect of long-term acute care for Anissa in a mental hospital was, her parents hoped Brookhaven would provide the kind of treatment she so desperately had needed for so long. The family deemed itself fortunate that her mother's IBM job provided good dependent health insurance coverage for Anissa to pay the hundreds of thousands of dollars Brookhaven eventually would charge for her care, never guessing that her having that insurance actually made Anissa the prey of a corrupt mental-health-care operation.

· · · · ·

Her first night at Brookhaven, the staff put Anissa into restraints.

She had become very upset as she considered what she faced. When Anissa was in Shoal Creek, her mother was just a short distance away and could arrive at the facility in a matter of minutes, if need be. Now her mother was a three- or four-hour drive away. Worse, Anissa had heard talk that Michael might be transferred to the IBM facility in Boca Raton, Florida, and her mother might be going with him. She panicked whenever she considered her mother might be removed from her by several states. She looked around at her surroundings at Brookhaven. She knew nothing about the staff, and they knew nothing about her. "Basically," she says, "they just handed me the rules and locked me in." It all overwhelmed her and she began weeping.

The staff tried to calm her. But at one point Anissa angrily threw a box of tissue. Anissa learned her first lesson about Brookhaven. The staff there placed its highest priority on control, so, in response to throwing the tissue box, Anissa wound up in restraints. Later, she heard from other juvenile patients that they thought she received a raw deal, being tied to a bed like that for such a minor infraction on her first night at Brookhaven. But raw deals, as it turned out, were the norm at Brookhaven. Making it all worse was the absence of the psychiatrist, Laurie Hellman,* who would be in charge of Anissa's care during her time at Brookhaven. Dr. Hellman was gone on vacation, so the psychiatrist who ordered the restraints wasn't familiar with Anissa's patient history.

For the infraction of throwing the tissue box, Anissa remained restrained to a bed for three days. She was terrified the whole time. At Shoal Creek, she'd been used to confinement in a room for misbehavior. But here they tied you down. Beyond immobilization, being in restraints also meant she had to use a bedpan for the first time in her life. She found this humiliating, and that became part of the punishment as well.

She went into restraints on a Friday. One Monday, she was examined by a psychiatrist who saw no need for her to be tied down. So she was freed. Later that week she met Dr. Hellman for the first time.

Dr. Hellman was an attractive woman roughly her mother's age, distinguished by her red hair and by a trace of an accent that suggested she might originally have come from someplace like the United Kingdom or Australia. She was well respected by her colleagues: At one point, she'd served as president of the American Society for Adolescent Psychiatry. She saw Dr. Hellman daily for at least fifteen minutes, and from their earliest sessions onward, Anissa believed she could trust her. Years later, after the Brookhaven scandal broke, Dr. Hellman was among the hospital staff members sued by former patients. And members of Anissa's family also would question whether Dr. Hellman truly acted in her best interests. But Anissa counted herself among the psychiatrist's loyalists — "Dr. Hellman's people." She liked and respected the woman, and she came to view her as something of a surrogate mother — "the most important person in my life at that time."

. . . . .

As Anissa settled into Brookhaven, much of her life focused on disputes with the staff and the punishments that followed:

> When I first got there, all they had were four-point restraints, you know, enough to tie down your hands and feet. All that other stuff came later — they ordered it as they needed it. At that point, the longest anyone had been in restraints was maybe two months. But that changed, largely because of me. I fought back so much that they had to get other forms of restraint. I was really bad. I mean, if they had me restrained with four-points, I'd do something like bite my shoulder, hard and deep, to injure myself.
>
> People came in to check on you once every fifteen minutes. There was always somebody in the hall, somebody in the day-room, no matter what activity was going on. They had their clipboards with them. They'd find you, make sure you were where you were supposed to be. When they checked on you, they asked if you needed something to drink, needed to go to the bathroom, that kind of stuff. They also gave you range of motion every two hours in which they'd take each of your limbs and move them around. It wasn't like you were hauled off some-

where when you went on restraints. You were in your room on the unit. You didn't have television or radio or anything. You were on restriction; it was punishment, you know?

I had roommates, and they'd been around mental hospitals for years. It wasn't like they were new to all this, not like my roommates at Shoal Creek who were there for a while then out. When I was on full restraints, most of my roommates hated me—well, they didn't hate me, they just didn't like rooming with me because my condition limited what they could do. It was a hassle for them. I mean, they might have been among the best-behaved patients there, but because they roomed with me, they'd have to deal with a lot of things being locked up. Like all the pencils and stuff in the room, they had to be locked up just in case I got loose and grabbed one to use as a weapon. So every time they wanted to write a letter, they'd have to get someone on staff to come into the room and unlock the pencils. And, of course, staff was always in there watching me, and having that person always present must have really annoyed my roommates. They didn't have nearly as much freedom as when they roomed with someone else.

Depending on what level of restraints you were on, you could do a lot of the things the other kids could. You could do your schoolwork. They'd loosen your hand or whatever to allow you to write. And you were on the same food schedule as the rest of the unit. They'd bring you breakfast when the others were having their breakfast and so on. You were pretty much doing the same thing as everyone else. They'd wheel your bed into group, all of that. But you were in restraints.

At first, it wasn't really such a big deal because people weren't in restraints for long enough for it to become an issue. You'd be in maybe a couple of days—maybe bed restraints for a day and then they'd move you to wheelchair restraints, where you're tied to a wheelchair but able to roll yourself around. That way, you can go to the activities. You go to school, you go eat in the kitchen, you go to everything, but your hands are tied. Then, the next step: It could be a day later, and you're in the wheelchair in the morning, and then the doctor comes in and talks to you and says, "Let her out." And then you're out of restraints. It was a step thing. You went from bed to wheelchair to freedom. But as time went on, the length of time people spent in restraints seemed to grow longer.

There were things to do. In a way, it was no different than not being in restraints. They kept you involved. You go to school, you go to group, you go for your appointment with the doctors. But if you are acting out, like I was, you lay there and figured out ways to get out. That was my thing, you know?

You know, you might ask if I worked on what was the cause of my problem with the hospital staffers. To tell the truth, it was so much about my behavior that we didn't get down to the "real" problem. They couldn't get to that point because I wouldn't behave. I did talk about some stuff concerning my mom. I remember that. About how I'd make progress, then my mom would come along and undo everything I'd accomplished. But we never got too deep into it. You see, mostly it was about how I was trying to get my needs met through acting out as opposed to talking about what I needed. At that time, talking about it just never seemed to do any good. So I'd get physically violent. Then they'd subdue me and put me into restraints, and then, once I was tied down, we might talk about it a little. You know, like, Why are you upset? Why are you out of control? That kind of thing.

But we never got down to real answers. A lot of it was just about how I felt about myself. Maybe I was just trying to avoid that for so long because I felt so bad about myself. When I really got to that point, I would just lose it. That demon would awaken inside me and take control. And so it became all about losing it.

It was always anger or self-abuse or something like that. I would just kind of go off. We would talk about things, and then I wouldn't know how to express what I wanted to say, or else I'd just get upset about what we were talking about. I wouldn't want them to see me so upset, so I'd pick up a chair and throw it or something. And finally the anger just takes over and stays in control.

Like I say, I was acting out in that way from the get-go. I remember thinking that if I couldn't be the best, then I was going to be the best at being the worst. You know, that kind of thing. I was a handful, to put it mildly.

It's strange how you come to look at things. When they would take me down to be restrained, I'd fight like everything, you know? But in a way, it was rewarding. It was a way of getting attention, you see? Almost a form of affection. Even while I was fighting them, I'd have it in my mind that they were doing this to keep me safe—just like when you're a kid, you're always wanting your parents to keep you safe. My mom always made desiring attention sound like a bad thing. That was weird, because when she was young, she wanted attention really bad. But with me, she acted like it was something negative. The truth is, everybody wants attention, everybody wants to be liked, everybody wants to be loved. And in my mind, I processed being restrained as a kind of act of unconditional love. I was thinking, They're doing this to me because they're worried about me. And, again in a weird way, being restrained was kind of like getting a really big hug, and that's what I wanted so much, to be hugged. But, you know, I was passing myself off as this really tough kid—I didn't act like I wanted hugging, and I'd sure as hell never outright ask for a hug. I was way too tough for that. I was like, Fuck you, I don't need any love or any attention or any of that. But I really did need it. And being restrained was a way of getting it all. And after I was restrained, I felt really secure. You can say how you hate it, how you hate being tied down, how you hate not even being able to take a pee when you need to. But at the same time, it was almost like I was back being an infant with adults taking care of me because I couldn't take care of myself. And I loved that part of it.

I don't know if I had the most problems in general of any kid there, but I can say without a doubt I had the most control problems, that's for sure. It was weird. I just kind of felt like I was there by myself. My parents were four hours away and didn't come to visit that often. Most of the kids there were from Dallas and their parents came for visiting hours during family night every Tuesday, bringing them treats from Taco Bell and stuff like that. I was just alone most of the time. Every six to eight weeks when my mom and my stepfather did come to visit—sometimes Roland came too; by this time, Ramon was away in the Marine Corps—their stays were always really short. Maybe they'd give me an hour's visit on Saturday and then they'd leave and go shopping or do whatever. On Sunday they'd come back for another hour. Then they'd be off for Austin and a couple of months would pass before I saw them again. And every visit was always supervised, you know, someone from Brookhaven was there. Who knows why?

The truth is, though, I was out of control, and I needed to be in restraints. It was obvious I needed to be there. As for the other kids at Brookhaven, I don't know. There were some who probably were treated more harshly than they deserved. But it's hard for me to say because I don't know to what extent they acted out.

But me, well, I was so angry about being there. And it came out. A typical incident might go like this: I'd be asked to do something or talk about something and I'd think, No, I'm not going to do it. Then one of the staffers would say, "Are you going to do it or not?" And I would just sit there. I can see them talking among themselves, talking and laughing. They'd say, "Okay, just go to your room." And I'd say, "No. I'm not going to my room. What do you plan to do about it?" And things would escalate from there and I'd shout, "Fuck you, why don't you go fuck your mother!" Stuff like that. You know, "Leave me alone and go fuck your mother some more!" And it would build from there until I threw a chair, screaming, "Fuck you all! Eat shit and die!" You see, it didn't have to go there. This might have all begun over something simple like me refusing to do my school-work, nothing more than that. But I would take it to someplace that was entirely inappropriate.

CHAPTER THREE | 55

Then you'd hear the intercom calling for "Dr. Rush." Of course, there was no Dr. Rush. That was the code for an emergency with a patient who'd gone out of control, a patient who needed to be "rushed," just like at Shoal Creek. So an emergency psychiatric team would show ready to subdue me so I could be restrained. And I'd resist them, of course, not really meaning to hurt anyone. As I resisted, I might have punched or kicked someone, maybe even bit or scratched some, but I didn't do it to hurt that person. I was just resisting.

Eventually, however, she did begin directing violence toward the staff, with the intent of hurting them. While at times Anissa got along with him well enough, at other times she viewed a technician named Thomas* as an enemy. At those times Thomas seemed to take a sadistic glee in upsetting patients and he particularly liked to pick on Anissa. One day, during a period of prolonged restraint, the staff rolled Anissa's bed into the hallway at night to make it easier for them to keep an eye on her. For whatever reason, they put her bed under a light, so she wasn't able to sleep well. Her room during the day was actually dimmer than the hall at night. So, tired from not being able to get much sleep in the hall, she'd often nod off during the day while in her room. But sleeping during the day violated the rules, never mind that she was pinned to a bed and couldn't do much of anything else (no TV, no music, nothing). Thomas loved to catch her napping. Instead of just rousing her, he liked to sneak up to her bed, kick it, and shout, "No sleeping!" Anissa would awaken with a start, her heart pounding rapidly, and see Thomas with a sickening grin on his face. After he did this several times, she began plotting to get revenge—"he was a true jackass."

She saw her opportunity one day when the unit was having a cookout in a courtyard for the patients who were not on restriction. So most of the kids and the staff were outside. Only two or three patients and Thomas remained inside. Anissa had been well behaved all day, and maybe that's why Thomas was a little lax when he loosened one of her hands at mealtime. Anissa got her hand on a fork, and before Thomas knew what was happening, she stabbed him with it. Thomas began wrestling with her to retrieve the fork and Anissa fought him as fiercely as was possible with just one free hand. When she had her chance, she bit him, clamping down on him as hard as she could. Like a pit bull, she refused to turn loose. Her teeth tore through his flesh and his blood gushed over the both of them. Hospital staffers rushed him to a nearby emergency room.

After things settled down, Anissa realized she'd taken a giant step backward in her recovery. A violent attack on a hospital staff member was a bad thing, a very bad thing. But she also thought she had no other choice but to assault him, given the situation. So she felt a combination of regret and satisfaction. Still, she was overcome by the sinking realization that if things had devolved to the point of her doing violence to someone like Thomas, freedom from the hospital wasn't going to come anytime soon. She'd be in Brookhaven for a long, long time. Besides, she just felt regretful about treating people bad.

One thing about it, though. Thomas stayed away from her from that point on.

While Thomas may have been the only staff member she attacked physically, Anissa learned there were other ways to hurt people who worked at Brookhaven—and hurt them badly. She remembers a woman assigned to do one-on-one therapy with her. She and the woman had been very friendly until the day Anissa let her anger get the best of her. Anissa says, "Now, whoever did a one-on-one with you, that person just had to sit there and take whatever you said. They can't say anything back to you, and they aren't allowed to beat you up. So this one day, I was in a really bad place, and I knew the woman there to conduct the one-on-one had to listen to me." Anissa launched into an hour-long tirade, ending it by telling the woman that she planned to track her down after she got out of the hospital and slaughter her entire family. The woman was shaking and in tears by the time Anissa finished. "You see, I wanted to make people feel as bad as I was feeling. I mean, it made no sense. At that time, I was fifteen, maybe sixteen years old, and I'm in a mental hospital under lockdown, and, on top of that, I was in restraints. Realistically, how am I going to get out of all these restraints, find out where you live, go there, then chop up your kids and put them in a freezer? You know? But even if it's not a very realistic possibility, it hurts for any mother to have to sit there and listen to someone saying that kind of hurtful shit about your kids. I think I just wore everybody out." Anissa's relationship with the woman was never the same after that day. Anissa learned there were consequences for her out-of-control behavior.

At this time, Anissa went free-falling into a bleak abyss. "It turned into something a whole lot darker," she says. "I was in a really scary place. The loneliness and emptiness you feel when you're in that place is just overwhelming. The quiet was overwhelming." It was especially bad for her on weekends, when many of the kids, mostly from the Dallas–Fort Worth area with family nearby, had passes and were absent from the hospital. Anissa felt herself going out of control and engaged in a protracted battle against the Brookhaven staff.

In her need to exert some control over something, she turned to an old friend: hurting herself. In her earlier days of cutting, she'd used a razor to slice herself open. In the restrictive environment at Brookhaven, razors and knives, of course, were not readily available. The hospital staff's propensity toward physical restraint further compounded her inability to carve on herself. Nevertheless, she found means to spill her blood. "When I'd cut myself," she says, "I didn't know how to stop until the blood was dripping on the floor. For me, cutting was all about the sight of my blood. Once I could see it, I felt this sense of relief."

She found success despite the staff's best attempts to constrain her. She began to gouge or bite herself fiercely enough to start the blood flow. As the number and strength of the restraints increased, she relied more and more on her teeth. Human flesh, she discovered, is remarkably tough. Piercing it takes effort. At a point when she was restrained from the neck downward, she used a reasoned approach to satisfy her need to bleed. By tilting her face to one side and downward toward her shoulder, she could gnaw on her skin until she made a small opening. Then, grasping her skin with her teeth, she'd snap her head in the opposite direction, ripping open a wound deep enough to reveal muscle and other tissue below. Blood cascaded down her shoulder. At Brookhaven she inflicted wounds on herself so severe that they required weeks of treatment before they healed. Today, if you watch Anissa working out in a tank top, you will see scars on her arms and shoulders, not from injuries received in the boxing ring, but from the damage she inflicted on herself at Brookhaven.

Her scarred wrist is testimony to the worst damage she did to herself. She became adept at contorting her body while under the net, and one day she succeeded in positioning her arm where she could bite her wrist. Her teeth dug in so deeply that when she popped the skin free she could see blood vessels and tendons. And a lot of blood. The wound was so severe that a plastic surgeon was called in for consultation. Special treatments followed designed to keep the internal section of the injury moist so that healing could occur from the inside out.

In terms of being restrained, Anissa became the star of the juvenile unit at the hospital. From the four points used on her during her first day at Brookhaven, she quickly progressed to more and more tie-down points until finally she was confined by twenty-six of them. Even this kind of restraint failed when she totally lost control of herself. Eventually the staff members turned from standard cuff-type restraints to more restrictive methods, but Anissa's determination to damage herself continued to frustrate them. Eventually totally immobilized, she satisfied her need for blood by biting the insides of her mouth and chewing on her tongue. "That had them shrugging their shoulders," she says. "What do you do to stop that?"

What was to be a one-year confinement in long-term treatment stretched out to nearly three years. For eighteen months of that time, Anissa was tied down to a bed, much of the time under a Posey body restraint net, which stretched from her neck to her ankles, with leather cuffs for the upper arms, wrists, and ankles and cross-straps to attach to each side of the bed. But even the body net wasn't enough. The staff added additional straps.

As time moved on, the notion that she faced a lifetime in long-term care tortured her. Her mind traveled to strange places as she remained immobilized, often under fetid conditions, in her bed. She had virtually no bodily contact with any other human beings except when staff members arrived to perform the most perfunctory tasks—moving her limbs to ward off bedsores, feeding her, cleaning her. But she received no hugs, no loving touches. In this dire condition, she bonded with her Posey net in much the same way a child bonds with a security blanket. Years after she left Brookhaven, she would find herself craving the touch of her long-gone net.

Of course, Anissa was far removed from many of the life events that normally accompany the metamorphosis from a girl to a woman. At a time when most girls are learning the nuances of dating and other aspects of romantic love, she was secluded, bound to a bed. The rarity of visits from her family made her feel even more isolated. Anissa found herself thinking more and more frequently about suicide.

But an end to the nightmare emerged at last, in an unlikely way. One day out of the blue Dr. Hellman told Anissa that IBM's insurance company had requested that Anissa's diagnosis and treatment be reevaluated. Everything changed quickly after that. "Dr. Hellman was always up front with me about it," Anissa says. "IBM's insurance company was threatening Brookhaven at the time. It was like, 'Look, you need to do something different with this girl or we are not going to pay any more money.'" She remembers being examined by psychiatrists from New York, California, and Austin. They concluded treatment changes were necessary. The officials at Brookhaven decided it was time for her to go elsewhere.

Anissa was dazed by what occurred once the hospital determined she needed to be on a fast track for dismissal:

These people came up with these measurements, like, If you're good for thirty minutes or an hour, you get a star. And the more stars you get, the more rewards you get. I realized they'd suddenly put me on a completely different program from everybody else, and I was making "progress" a lot faster than everybody else. My stars were gathering up in a hurry. As rewards, they started taking straps off me. You know, they'd say, "You've been good, so you get one less strap." Then the next thing you know, they're taking another strap off. And then another. And then another. It was a real shock. I mean, I was actually getting sick a lot because I'd been tied down for so long that my body wasn't used to even doing little things like sitting up. It made me nauseous. And my body was in terrible shape otherwise. Like, my legs were so atrophied that there was no way I could do something as simple as run a little. Another thing: I never had any drug therapy because we understood that Brookhaven didn't believe in using drugs to treat patients. But once IBM threatened to stop paying, suddenly I was getting drug therapy too.

All these changes happened very quickly, like in the last three months I was at Brookhaven. I remember the last week I was there. I was still technically restrained, but by now restrained to a wheelchair instead of to a bed. And I only had one strap. On Monday of that week, they came in and told me I would be dismissed on Friday. It was that Friday morning when they finally removed the last restraint. And by that afternoon, I was discharged from Brookhaven.

Waiting for her the day she was dismissed were her mother and Michael, who drove her directly from Brookhaven to Charter Lane (a mental hospital no longer in business) in Austin. While traveling down Interstate 35, they reminded Anissa of their agreement to stay married for a minimum of five years. That time limit had expired. As she stared at the dismal fast food restaurants and motels that lined the highway, Anissa learned that her mother and Michael were divorcing. That made the trip to Austin bittersweet.

Sure, she was free from Brookhaven. But she saw ahead of her the loss of a stepfather who had been supportive and kind during her bleakest hours.

Still to come was a four-month stint at Charter Lane. She underwent serious culture shock when she arrived there. After three years of "major lockdowns" and dealing with "really serious stuff" at Brookhaven, she went to a hospital where the treatment was "superficial bullshit." She considered it a waste of her time in terms of her coming to grips with her demons. She remembers the staff there as being obsessively concerned with the most mundane of behavioral details—"for instance, like how you set your cup down after you'd finished drinking"—rather than addressing the bigger problems she faced.

Once the four months had passed, she graduated from Charter Lane to day treatment at St. David's Hospital in Austin. The therapy she received there did little good. "At that time," she says, "I was just so messed up. I was just gone. There wasn't enough time for me to get really acclimated back to anything resembling normal. Everything was just weird to me. Not only had I not been in touch with the world for years, I was, like, not really even in touch with any person. For instance, I didn't have relationships with other kids, you know? I didn't have relationships with friends. I'd just been tied to a bed. That's all. One thing I did during this time when I was living at home is get sheets and tie them together, then tie myself down with them, so I'd get that secure feeling I had when restrained at Brookhaven. It was just like being in four-point restraints. I'd do that because, really, that's all I'd known for so long. I'd feel *normal*, if you can believe that. Now that's twisted, but that's how it was for me."

During her treatment at St. David's, she hit a new low. Her violent behavior began increasing. One day she kicked a hole in a wall at the hospital, and the staff called the cops. She wound up committed by law to the Austin State Hospital. A sheriff's deputy led her away in handcuffs. After release from the state hospital, she went back to St. David's, only to find her problems with violence recurring. Another involuntary stay at the state hospital followed.

Around that time, she also slashed her wrists. Finally St. David's released her.

Education was all but lost in the hospital shuffle. Once she was released from St. David's, it was impossible for her to transition herself back into high school, although she did give it a try at Round Rock High School. In addition to realizing she trailed other students academically, she discovered she also lacked the basic social skills required to get through high school life. She didn't know how to get a friend or interact with people in general. She only understood how to express herself through violence. If something angered her, she could not say how she felt verbally. She had to hit someone to let people know she was mad. That, of course, did not play well at school.

Anissa moved with her mother to a duplex in Round Rock West, a housing development within easy walking distance of the high school, while Michael, soon to depart for New England, continued to live in the family's old house. Her mother had begun dating another man, and Anissa, who loved her stepfather, was angry about the new relationship. She disliked her mother's new boyfriend, and he was not particularly fond of her. Though the relationship was in its infancy, the new boyfriend was already complaining that Anissa's mother was paying too much attention to her and not enough to him. Anissa describes her behavior at this time as being "very psychotic. I was praying to the devil then, not to God. I wanted to kill my mother then, I was that angry with her, so filled with hate."

Aggravating the situation was a new habit Anissa had discovered. One day she found a can of gasoline in the garage. She unscrewed the cap and snorted the fumes. With that, she began a six-month binge of indulging in what's arguably the most dangerous of all forms of substance abuse—huffing. She soon graduated to smoking paint thinner in a pipe, doing it whenever she had a chance. For months she spent all her waking hours truly fucked up. She was so inebriated, she sometimes would walk into a neighbor's house, thinking it was her mother's place. One time she did this and the neighbor reacted by gently turning her around by the shoulders, pointing at her mother's duplex, and saying, "No, honey, you live over there." Zombielike, Anissa said, "Oh, okay," and walked home in the rain. Round Rock High School eventually expelled her and Anissa would stay at home, huffing the day away while her mother worked.

Shortly she was back in a hospital, this time ICU. From there, she went directly into drug rehab at Shoal Creek. She'd just turned eighteen and was the youngest person in the adult rehab unit. She found that she had nothing in common with the other patients in the unit, most of whom seemed to her to be male executive-type people who were being treated for alcohol and cocaine abuse. She thought of herself as the strange punk-ass kid in the group who'd been huffing paint thinner while the others were doing high-price powder cocaine at expensive nightclubs. "I would listen during group therapy," she says. "I loved to tell all those older guys to fuck off." She cut her wrists and ended up in PICU for a full month.

But a surprising thing occurred while she was in Shoal Creek. When she came out of her stay in PICU, her head began to clear. She describes it as something inside her clicking; she understood she needed to get her shit together or else she could face a life-time in mental hospitals, a lifetime of the hell she experienced at Brookhaven. She began making progress quickly. Her mother had reached the point where she believed she could no longer put up with Anissa—by this time, her now former stepfather, Michael, instead of her mother, was her primary visitor at Shoal Creek. Her family discussed her situation and decided that she should live once more with her father, who had moved back to San Angelo. So Anissa traveled back to the West Texas city where she'd spent her happy early years. It was one of the best things that ever happened to her.

CHAPTER FOUR

I think West Texas is exactly where I should have been.
Everything is kind of turned down low out there, you know
what I mean? There's not a lot going on, and that's exactly
what I needed. All the loud noises, all the doctors, all the
excitement, stress—it was all gone.

—ANISSA

. . . . .

Anissa's father had gone through his own rough times following the divorce from her mother. He left Austin and lived
in different towns before going home to San Angelo, where he
moved in with Anissa's grandparents and began trying to establish
his own insurance agency. Living with her father meant getting to
know his family and developing a sense of her roots. She thrived as
she did so and she felt better than she had in a very long time—no
recreational drugs, no huffing, no psychiatric drugs, no doctors
dredging stuff out of dark places. Everything around her seemed
to have slowed down, and that was good. It gave her a chance to
clear her head. For the first time, she sensed that she could be in
charge of herself, that she didn't have to give in to angry impulses.
She felt relieved by that. She was so weary of feeling out of control. It had gone on for too many years. "I think a lot of it was me
maturing too," she says, "becoming a grown-up instead of a way-
out-of-control teenager."

While staying with her father and his family, she heard stories
about how it was for them as Mexican Americans in West Texas
during earlier times. She learned that her grandparents' generation
never got to go to school for the full academic year; kids would be

pulled from classes to join their parents as migrant farmworkers, traveling hundreds and hundreds of miles throughout the United States as they followed the harvest. It was essential for survival of the family. She also learned about the hard work her father had been required to do after school and on weekends at her grandfather's auto repair shop. Through these kinds of stories, she got a sense of what her family members had been through and why circumstances had developed as they had.

Best of all, she grew close to her grandmother. Her grandmother spoke no English, and Anissa, of course, spoke no Spanish. Yet they were able to communicate with each other. Anissa detected no negative judgment from her grandmother, despite all Anissa had been through. She just felt love, love that manifested itself in small yet sublime ways. For instance, when making oatmeal for grandchildren, her grandmother stirred Nestlé's Quik into each bowl to add a little chocolate treat to breakfast. Her grandmother was a giver, and among the gifts Anissa received from her were sweaters and towels. The sweaters were "old lady" sweaters that Anissa would never wear, but she's held on to them for years and plans never to turn loose of them. The sentimental value behind them is too great.

Her paternal grandfather was still alive, but he suffered from Parkinson's disease and dementia, so it was not really possible for her to become as close to him. From members of her mother's family, she'd always heard very bad things about her father's father. In spite of his illnesses, she was able to learn that he was something other than a monster. Sometimes she helped take care of him, bathing him, brushing his teeth, combing his hair. Often the results were comical. She remembers one time when, after she'd finished sprucing him up for the day, he turned and said to her, "I think I can go to the bar now."

She took mental notes on all she heard and saw during those nine months in San Angelo. She witnessed how love can help people heal themselves. She also witnessed the destructive power of hate as she contemplated how much energy some of the people she knew in San Angelo wasted on anger and in finding fault with people. She pondered these things and considered all she'd been through and all she'd missed in life.

Determined to get the most out of living that she could, she was ready to return to Austin. But there was some unfinished business: her education. Her mother had laid down some requirements before she'd let Anissa live with her in Austin. First, she had to get a high school diploma. Second, she had to have a job.

"I tried some self-paced schools in an attempt to get my high school diploma," Anissa says. "But it wasn't working out. Finally, my dad said, 'I'm tired of this shit.' He just took me down to get my GED. I took the test, passed it, and suddenly I had my equivalency degree. So there was one goal achieved."

She moved to Austin, where a temp agency found her work at her mom's old employer, Texas Instruments, then, later at Abbott Laboratories' large pharmaceutical plant. Abbott soon offered her a permanent position. She was anxious to get on with her life. She didn't know much about checking accounts or some of the other necessities of day-to-day life (she depended on her brother Roland for help in these matters), but she knew she was ready to have fun. No city in America can offer more to a young person anxious to cut loose and party down than Austin. An old saw holds that no one who actually lives in Austin—at least no one beyond a certain age—would be caught dead after dark in the famed entertainment district on Sixth Street east of Congress Avenue, but to a budding Anissa, who had lost too many years in mental hospitals, Sixth Street offered plenty of opportunities for fun.

Within a relatively short time she had a steady boyfriend, with whom she eventually shared an apartment. As would be the case in future romantic involvements, her boyfriend was older than she, which eventually contributed to the relationship's demise, but for a time they enjoyed partying and living together. In addition to that with her boyfriend, she cultivated another relationship: She found a great connection for powder cocaine. Because she had money in her pocket from her job, she could afford the drug, and she was not shy about indulging herself. Other drugs played roles in her life at this time. She became reacquainted with marijuana, and a friend with whom she worked at Abbott introduced her to locally cultivated psilocybin, or psychedelic mushrooms. But she developed a passion for coke—"from my first taste, I was pretty much totally into it." Things began to go awry with her boyfriend. Anissa owns up to cheating on him. It was easy enough to do, with coke as the focus of her life instead of the relationship.

"The thing is," she says, "when you're doing a lot of coke, all you really care about is scoring and getting back to your apartment and doing more of it. The coke is more important than the people in your life or anything else. I was always on coke. Everything in my life was surrounded by and shaped by coke. I'd go to parties, and they were all about doing coke. The people I hung with, they were all doing coke."

To be sure, she was having fun, but she sensed her life was slipping out of control. She needed to make some changes. For one thing, her relationship with her boyfriend wasn't working out, even if she felt a measure of affection toward him. It wasn't an easy thing to confront. She wept telling him that she had to end their relationship, but she understood she had to do it. She also began to distance herself from her acquaintances who devoted their free time to snorting blow. She knew things were going to end in a bad way if she kept going down the scoring-and-partying path.

Around this same time, she took up karate with an earnestness she'd not shown toward the martial art since her adolescence. She found satisfaction in it, just as she had all those years earlier. But she also injured herself. It turned out she'd torn an anterior cruciate ligament (ACL). She explored options to karate, looking for something that might be easier on her knees, and that took her one day to a small boxing gym tucked behind a Goodwill store in a blue-collar section of central Austin. The place intrigued her, but she learned fast that boxing would be no easier on her knees than karate. She had surgery on the torn ACL and went on one last partying jag as she recovered. But she never forgot that boxing gym.

. . . . .

One day, Anissa's telephone rang and she was astonished to hear the voice of Clayton,* who had been a patient with her at Brookhaven. Though she'd worked hard to distance herself from that ugly phase of her life, she wasn't unhappy Clayton had called. They'd been friends at the hospital. She enjoyed catching up on what was happening in Clayton's life and recounting old times at "Heaven"—the pun on the hospital's name used by former patients—and in general cutting up over the phone.

"Excuse me," said the voice of an older man, interrupting their conversation.

Suddenly Clayton became quiet. Anissa was confused. The man continued, explaining that he was Clayton's attorney, and while he was glad Clayton and Anissa were enjoying talking to each other, that was not the real purpose of the call.

"So what's this about?" Anissa said.

The attorney said he represented Clayton and other former Brookhaven patients in lawsuits against the hospital, its parent company, and its staff. He talked about the long period Anissa spent bound to a bed. "It was wrong," he told her. He encouraged her to consider becoming a plaintiff herself. If she successfully sued, she stood to get a considerable amount of money.

Anissa hung up feeling anxious, confused, angry. She also felt betrayed and manipulated by the way the attorney had used his client Clayton to get access to Anissa. Now she had a big decision to make.

. . . . .

In the years since Anissa's release from Brookhaven, which went out of business amid scandal in 1992, hundreds of youthful former patients of the hospital and other facilities operated by Psychiatric Institutes of America/National Medical Enterprises had sued the company, alleging they were held prisoner for their insurance money. At one point in the 1990s, 250 suits, some with multiple plaintiffs, were pending—27 of those in Texas, involving Brook-haven and sister facilities in Fort Worth and Conroe. And this was *after* the company had already settled wrongful hospitalization ac-tions filed in Fort Worth and Conroe by some 700 former patients. The *New York Times* reported the settlement at $100 million. Later reports state that the company eventually spent $232.4 million on civil suit payouts.

Moreover, the Texas attorney general's office had reviewed a staggering 800 psychiatric cases in an investigation of the abuse scandal. Federal prosecutors also investigated, and in the end, some psychiatrists lost their medical licenses, while two doctors were convicted on criminal charges. PIA/NME as a corporation eventually pleaded guilty to federal conspiracy charges for pay-ing kickbacks and bribes to psychiatrists, psychologists, and other medical professionals from at least 1986 through 1991. Pete Alexis, a regional PIA/NME officer, admitted to paying out between $20 million and $40 million in bribes for patient referrals to Texas psy-chiatric hospitals run by the company. (In an agreement to settle a civil suit, Alexis agreed to give up more than $200,000 in assets, including a collection of Cartier jewelry, furs, antiques, and art, ac-cording to the *Houston Chronicle*.) In all, PIA/NME paid a record fine of $379 million, the largest fine ever paid for medical health-care fraud. It also made settlements with insurance companies, as well as with company shareholders whose investments plummeted once the scandal broke. (In 1995, NME changed its name to Tenet Healthcare after a merger with American Medical Holdings Inc.)

The reported settlements with and judgments for individual plaintiffs in the flurry of lawsuits involving Brookhaven and other NME hospitals ranged from $8.4 million to several hundred thou-sand dollars. Anissa's involvement in the litigation as one of the "star" patients of imprisonment and restraint held out the possi-bility of making her a lot of money.

One of the names that recurred in the list of defendants in the suits (as well as in the list of plaintiffs in suits filed by psychia-trists alleging defamation and against PIA/NME alleging finan-cial harm) was Laurie Hellman, although Dr. Hellman apparently never faced criminal charges connected with Brookhaven. At this point Anissa was still driving to Dallas on a fairly regular basis to receive treatment from Dr. Hellman, as well as consulting with her by telephone. Dr. Hellman was not charging Anissa for these services.

. . . . .

She dialed Dr. Hellman's number not long after talking to Clayton and the attorney.

"What's going on?" Anissa asked her, after telling her about the conversation she'd had. "What's this all about?"

For a moment or two, Dr. Hellman could only say, "Oh Anissa, oh Anissa." She sounded distraught to Anissa. Then she began explaining her take on the situation. "The way she made it sound," Anissa says, "was like the people suing were just being wimpy about everything, just trash-talking and saying they were so mistreated. Of course, I didn't want to be known as a bellyacher. And I started thinking about some of the kids who were suing, and I kind of thought, Oh, they're doing a poor, poor pitiful me trip. And I thought, If anyone should be suing, it should be me! You know, if someone is going to get away with this, let it be me. But, you know, deep down I felt like I was responsible for the bad stuff I did. I got myself into that mess by acting out, by reacting so violently to things. Now, it was their responsibility—the people at the hospital's responsibility—to look after me after I was in the mess. They were getting paid to do that. To be honest, I know they tried."

Anissa told Dr. Hellman she didn't want to be involved in the lawsuit, that she didn't even want to hear from Clayton's lawyer again. Dr. Hellman volunteered to contact her attorney to inform him that Anissa wanted no further contact with lawyers representing plaintiffs in the Brookhaven litigation. Anissa never heard from Clayton or his lawyer again.

Anissa says, "Now, you talk to my family, they wanted me to go through with it. My brother Roland is still angry about it. He and the rest of them all think it was the stupidest thing that I have ever done, not suing. He'll say, 'You know, Anissa, I knew what they were doing to you at Brookhaven was wrong, but I was just too young to do anything about it. I was really still a kid, but every time we came and saw you, I knew it was wrong.'

"Roland has a point. Since the lawsuits ended, I haven't heard a peep from Dr. Hellman. I can't tell you today where to find her. But you know, none of Dr. Hellman's true people sued, those of us who got something out of our interaction with her. Most of my roommates didn't sue. I kept seeing Dr. Hellman after I left Brookhaven mostly because I missed her. As I said, she had become sort of like a mom to me while I was there. I didn't want to hurt her. The last time I talked to her was after one of the former patients from Brookhaven died. She was really hesitant about talking to me until she figured out I wasn't coming back to see her. Then everything was okay. You know, the doctors sued some of the patients who made allegations against them, and they sued Brookhaven too for damaging their career. All those lawsuits, everybody suing everybody else, it made everyone suspicious and jittery. That's too bad."

In spite of what her family and friends thought, Anissa had no regrets about not suing.

Anissa learned that many of the former patients she knew who won suits or received settlements did not end up with the best of lives. In fact, some did not even live for very long. One friend used some of his money to buy a high-powered sports car, which he promptly wrecked at a high speed, killing himself. A young woman who'd been a patient at Brookhaven died as the victim of homicide. So Anissa was glad to distance herself from that time and place, even if it cost her a lot of money.

On the other hand, she wasn't ready to settle down to a "normal" life. All around her she saw people who had fallen into a trap: You grow up, you get a job, you come home and flop down on the couch in front of the TV, beer in hand, and complain about how work sucks. The days, weeks, months, and years all run together, and one day you look around and two decades have passed and you realize life has passed you by and you haven't accomplished much of anything except sit on the couch and complain. Anissa dreaded the prospect of living this way.

But a life of partying wasn't the answer either—she'd devoted enough of her energies to that with nothing to show for it. She believed there had to be something more.

CHAPTER FIVE

*From the get-go, I liked the hard work you did at the gym.
I mean, I liked it a lot. It was something I found that finally
pushed me. Now, it wasn't all Jim Dandy from the moment
I walked into the gym. But it wasn't long before I realized
that for the first time I'd found the thing I'd been looking
for. I felt a challenge, deep down in my gut, and
that challenge pushed me.*

—ANISSA

. . . . .

R ichard Lord moves with athletic grace—with good reason.
He's been an athlete all his life. He first entered the ring as
an amateur boxer when he was still in grade school in the 1960s
and later won Golden Gloves titles. Now, in his fifties, he is as lean
as he was back in the early 1980s when he fought professionally
in super featherweight and lightweight matches at a time when
champs like Roberto Duran, Alexis Arguello, Esteban De Jesus,
and Ray "Boom Boom" Mancini drew a great deal of attention to
boxing's lighter divisions. Eventually boxing authorities rated him
the number eight contender for the super featherweight title, although he never had the opportunity to win it. He kept a promise
to his mother to quit boxing when he turned thirty and ended his
boxing career with an all but spotless record of fourteen wins, one
loss, and one draw. He also ended his career with a boxer's broken
nose—and an enduring fascination with the sport.

Richard grew up in Dallas, where his father, Doug Lord, is
something of a local legend. Doug and his wife, Opal, were raised
in the Masonic Home and School in Fort Worth. During the

1930s, the Masonic Home's football squad of orphans proved to be one of the most dominant teams in the cutthroat realm of Texas high school football, and Doug was a team standout. Later he became an insurance executive and also gained a reputation in some quarters for his skill at hypnosis. But he was best known around Dallas as a boxing manager and promoter. In the 1960s, he guided one of his fighters, Curtis Cokes, to the world welterweight championship. It was an impressive accomplishment for both boxer and manager. Doug was an independent, far removed from New York, the center of boxing in America. He was not affiliated with any big-name management crews or a famous gym like Gleason's. Such entities made up a kind of power structure within professional boxing that exerted control over world titles and the boxers who held them. But Doug and Cokes came from the outside, and for three years Cokes held the title, unbeholden to the big names in the sport.

When Richard made the transition from boxer to manager and trainer, he followed his father's lead and avoided entangling himself with boxing's power brokers. As a champion, Cokes was famous for the strict conditioning regimen to which he adhered under Doug's direction. Like Cokes, Richard believed that fanaticism about conditioning was the foundation for boxing success, and he stuck to an astonishing training program. He would impart that fanaticism to boxers like Anissa and Jesus Chavez who trained under him in years to come. Richard's big dream was to guide a fighter to a world championship and do it the same way his father had done it—from the outside, with a boxer whose superb physical conditioning would give him an edge over his opponent.

Both during and after his boxing career, Richard involved himself in several business ventures, all the while maintaining his interest in training boxers. Lord fought many of his fights at the old Austin Coliseum, so he was well known in his adopted hometown. This helped him make connections in the business community. For a time, he ran a pizzeria in South Austin, where people passing by on the sidewalk could be entertained by the cook twirling dough in the storefront window. A regular at the pizzeria was a guitarist then hardly known outside Austin. Stevie Ray Vaughan was a big fan of the carrot cake that Richard sold as a dessert, and he'd stop by for a piece in the wee hours just before the pizzeria's late-night closing time. Later, rock star David Bowie hired Richard to teach him boxing and help him get in shape for the *Let's Dance* tour. Richard decamped to Dallas to train the erstwhile Thin White Duke and consort with Bowie's minions, one of whom turned out to be Vaughan. Bowie had hired Stevie Ray to play both on the hit album and in his touring band. As the band rehearsed one day in Dallas, Vaughan spotted Richard and announced that the fitness expert made one outstandingly decadent carrot cake. Soon Richard was baking treats for members of the band.

Richard's first gym was located on the second floor of a building in downtown Austin, just off Sixth Street. He eventually closed this gym and went back into the restaurant business, working with Eddie Wilson at Threadgill's, the eatery of Wilson's housed in the legendary old filling station–cum–beer joint where Janis Joplin started her singing career in the 1960s. Wilson had rented storage space in a warehouse development on Lamar Boulevard several blocks south of Threadgill's. The buildings that made up the development yielded any semblance of style to functionality: prefabricated metal exteriors, concrete floors, garage-type overhead doors. Wilson had rented storage space in a single long building divided up into bays. Each bay was accessible through an overhead door large enough to accommodate a truck or through a simple metal pedestrian door. There were no windows. While the building was wired for electricity and plumbed, the landlord did not provide air-conditioning or heating. If a tenant wanted such luxuries, he or she was responsible for installing it. Wilson had rented a single bay, and since it was used for storage, he saw no need to heat or cool it.

Eventually Wilson and Richard parted company, and Richard took over this Spartan storage area to house his second gym. Starting with this small space—over the years, the gym tripled in size, occupying three bays—Richard became a full-time boxing trainer, manager, and promoter by the early 1990s.

One thing set Richard apart from many of his contemporaries in boxing. From his earliest exposure to the sport, women had been involved. In fact, his sister trained at the boxing gym in Dallas, learning to fight as Richard himself discovered the finer points of the sweet science. Throughout the remainder of his career, he saw women working out alongside male boxers, even if there were no organized boxing competitions at the time in which these female athletes could compete. So he thought it perfectly normal for women to be part of boxing.

Richard's decision to commit himself to boxing as a trainer, manager, and promoter in the early 1990s corresponded with a sudden burst of interest in women's boxing. Christy Martin fought her first pro match in 1989 and soon would garner national attention as a boxer. Meanwhile, Dallas Malloy became the first female boxer to challenge the prohibition against women in the bylaws of USA Boxing Inc., the sport's leading amateur sanctioning organization. Her lawsuit, filed in U.S. District Court in Seattle, resulted in Judge Barbara Rothstein's issuing a restraining order against USA Boxing Inc., thus opening the door for women in amateur boxing.

Given Richard's background and these developments on the boxing scene, it seemed only natural that he begin training and promoting female boxers, welcoming the opportunity to bring a new dimension to the sport even as many boxing mainstays like Tony Ayala were voicing their opposition to women in the ring. In 1993, he promoted the first all-female boxing match sanctioned by USA Boxing Inc. Proceeds went to the Austin Rape Crisis Center. The next year, Austin Mayor Bruce Todd honored Richard for his efforts to empower women through boxing by naming March 31 "Richard Lord Day."

Anissa began training in earnest at Richard's gym in 1993 in the midst of these exciting developments in the world of women's boxing. She remembers her very first day there. She went alone, unsure of what she'd find. As she stepped in through the open overhead door, she spied three or four women working out. It was a complete surprise to her. She didn't think women would be training there.

. . . . .

In fact, when Anissa first slipped her fist into a boxing glove, she became part of a long, if unheralded, tradition. Women's boxing has roots that can be traced back nearly three hundred years, back to the days when sports enthusiasts in England were reviving the long dormant sport that had originated with the ancient Greeks.

In its online history of the sport, the Women Boxing Archive Network reports that women's boxing matches occurred in London in the 1720s, although they scarcely resembled boxing as it's now practiced. In those bouts in Georgian England, the female pugilists not only threw punches but also kneed, kicked, scratched, gouged, mauled, and pulled the hair of their opponents. Winners and losers alike frequently left the ring with serious injuries. The matches were staged before paying audiences, and apparently a system recognizing the best boxers was in place. One report from 1722 states that a fight between two women occurred at Boarded House (near present-day Oxford Circus) and starred Elizabeth Wilkinson, "the Cockney Championess." Wilkinson defeated Martha Jones to retain her Cockney title.

The first recorded female boxing match in the United States took place at the Hills Theater in New York City in 1876. Nell Saunders and Rose Harland met in the ring to compete for a prize of a silver butter dish. Though records are scant, one can assume that at least scattered occurrences of women's boxing continued to take place in America through the end of the nineteenth century and into the twentieth century, for female boxers took part in demonstration matches at the 1904 Olympics in St. Louis. In the 1920s, some physical education instructors included boxing as part of their fitness programs for young women in Boston. But for the most part, women's boxing lay dormant in America through the twentieth century; in some states, fights between women were illegal. Still, a few matches took place, although the public generally accorded them no more respect than that usually given to circus sideshows.

One compelling female boxer was Barbara Buttrick, who for a time in the 1950s fought out of Dallas as "the Mighty Atom of the Ring." She was born and reared in the United Kingdom, where she began boxing as a 4′11″, 98-pound flyweight, according to a 1998 profile of her in the *Miami Herald*. "I was small, but I was mean," she told the newspaper, words that seem appropriate for Anissa as well. Buttrick began fighting in the UK, inspired by a newspaper account she'd read of an early-twentieth-century female British boxer named Polly Burns. Buttrick bought gloves and a book entitled *The Noble Art of Self-Defense* and began working with a trainer. She spent her days clicking the keys of a typewriter in a London office, then trained three hours every evening: skipping rope, sparring, working the bags. Eventually she married her coach, Len Smith, and began touring the small towns, fighting in "booths"—small portable rings. British rules prohibited women participating in boxing, so her matches were strictly off the books. Her fights were more carnival-like. The booth would be set up in a small English town and word would be spread that she was available to take on any challengers. One trip took her across the channel to France, where she fought fifteen two-round exhibition matches in a single day.

In 1952, she and Smith moved to the United States, where she won eight straight fights and knocked out an opponent who was recognized by some people as America's female bantamweight champion. In 1957, she moved to Dallas. She and rival Phyllis Kugler received state-accredited boxing licenses, a first for Texas. The two fought in a bout staged in San Antonio as a world championship match. Buttrick won and is credited in some corners as the first-ever female world boxing champion. By that point, she'd fought a thousand exhibition matches against men and taken part in eighteen women's professional fights, winning all but one: She lost to an opponent who outweighed her by thirty-three pounds; Buttrick also was suffering from the flu at the time.

She and Smith moved to Florida in the late 1950s, where she trained at the Fifth Street Gym, later to become famous as Muhammad Ali's training base. Four months pregnant, she fought her last fight in 1960. She went on to become a noted ringside photographer, and she founded the Women's International Boxing Federation in 1993. She continues to serve as that organization's president.

Fascinating as Buttrick's career was, it took place at a time when women's prizefighting was not an organized sport, when only a handful of women had even the slightest training in boxing, when a legitimate system of ranking opponents and recognizing champions still lay far in the future. Interest in women's boxing began to gain real momentum in the 1970s with the flowering of the women's movement and the corresponding celebration of the success women were beginning to achieve in nontraditional roles. In January 1975, Eva Shain became the first woman licensed to judge professional boxing. Two years later, she was one of three judges scoring the heavyweight match between champion Muhammad Ali and contender Earnie Shavers, the first time a woman was to judge a world title fight. The attention given to Shain's work outside the ring helped spur the interest in women actually lacing on gloves and climbing through the ropes.

Also in 1975, Caroline Svendsen received the first documented professional boxer's license ever granted to a woman in the United States. She fought in a sanctioned four-round fight in Virginia City that same year. The next year, Pat Pineda received her pro license in California. It took a lawsuit to accomplish it, but in 1978 Cathy "Cat" Davis, Jackie Tonawanda, and Marian "Lady Tyger" Trimiar became licensed professional fighters in the American Mecca of boxing, New York. Other women in jurisdictions across the country found themselves successful in becoming licensed pros in the late 1970s. And in 1978, Cat Davis made the cover of *The Ring* magazine, boxing's self-anointed Bible. The resulting furor shook the boxing world like nothing had since that day in Houston more than ten years earlier when Muhammad Ali refused to step forward for the military draft.

Although Davis was a groundbreaker, she also found herself involved in a scandal that helped slow the progress of women's boxing. Claims that the outcomes of some of her matches were rigged
cast doubt on the sport as a whole and showed the need for legitimate governing/sanctioning organizations, meaningful licensing
processes, and upright refereeing and judging of women's fights.
As late as 1987, the Lady Tyger felt the need to go on a hunger
strike (losing thirty pounds in the process) to call attention to the
sorry state of women's boxing. "Unless women get more recognition," she said, "we will be fighting just as a novelty for the rest of
our lives. There will be no future."

But by the time Anissa started boxing in the early 1990s, the
sport was attracting female athletes determined to make it more
than just a novelty.

. . . . .

Two of the women she met early on at the gym were Lori Lazarine
and Amy Miller (now Simmons). Lori was a nurse who'd come to
boxing by way of karate; shortly she would marry Richard Lord
and fight under her married name, Lori Lord. Amy was rapidly
becoming one of Austin's best-known businesswomen. After aban-
doning early aspirations of becoming a physician, Amy entered the
gourmet ice cream business in Manhattan and Florida. In 1984,
she and her then–business partner, Scott Shaw, opened Amy's Ice
Creams on Guadalupe in Austin. At the time, the business was
on shaky enough ground that the first month's rent was paid for
with a hot check. But Amy's Ice Creams soon became a popular
destination for Austinites with a sweet tooth, and eventually the
business would grow to include more than a half dozen locations
in Austin, plus stores in Houston and San Antonio. Ironically,
Amy the ice cream entrepreneur was also a dedicated fitness buff
who had been a competitive gymnast and ran marathons. She and
Lori applied for professional boxer's licenses simultaneously, and
on January 19, 1993, they fought in the Rio Grande Valley town of

McAllen in Texas's first women's professional boxing match of the sport's modern era. Lori, who would box professionally for seven more years, won the four-round decision.

Anissa watched Amy and Lori work out and learned about their foray into professional boxing. The notion of entering the ring herself intrigued her. But she was out of shape and knew nothing about prizefighting. She settled into Richard's tough training routine not knowing just where this all might end up.

She worked the third shift at Abbott Laboratories, leaving her job in the early morning. Three days a week she'd drive directly from Abbott to Hyde Park Gym to join Richard and other boxers in strength training with free weights. Usually she arrived before Richard and the others showed up, so she'd sleep for a while in her car. After lifting, she'd go home and sleep until two in the afternoon before heading to Richard's gym for daily boxing training, which usually lasted for a couple of hours. She also ran every day. Then she'd return to her job at Abbott.

"I felt a challenge deep down in my gut," she says about her grueling schedule. "That challenge pushed me. It was hard to keep up. But Richard kept saying, 'You're doing all right.' It was hard, yes, but it was just what I needed in my life."

Richard, of course, had no idea what Anissa had been through during her teenage years nor the specifics of her partying years. During her early days in the gym, he saw in her a young woman who'd been treating herself to the hedonistic side of life while ignoring the benefits of intense physical training. But he began to detect something else the more he was around her.

The physical components of boxing success are important. But even the most skilled boxer in the best of shape won't triumph in the ring unless she has the right psychological makeup too. Part of it is willpower. She must have the ability to force herself to continue battling even when her mind is telling her to quit—ignore the voice saying that the task is too great, that the pain from her opponent's blows is too much to bear. But beyond that, a boxer must also carry with her pent-up aggression that can be released when the bell clangs. A boxer must be willing to hurt another person; moreover, she must receive some satisfaction in doing so. In short, to use Richard's term for it, she must have a "mean streak."

If you hang around a boxing gym, you'll find athletic women in great shape who have learned many of the fundamentals through mitt drills, shadowboxing, and training on the speed, vertical, and heavy bags. But for whatever reason, they decline to take the next step: donning protective gear and stepping into the ring to spar. They can't find the wherewithal to hit another woman.

For Anissa, however, it was not a problem. Richard saw she had the mean streak.

Anissa remembers that she had been to the gym no more than a half dozen times at most when she asked Richard when she could begin sparring. Richard responded by saying, "Let's see if you can show me a one-two-slip." It's the simplest combination a boxer learns. For a right-hander like Anissa, it involves throwing a jab with the left hand (the "one" in the combination) to set up the right-cross power punch ("two"). After throwing the right, the boxer "slips" the anticipated counterpunch from her opponent by bending her knees to lower her body out of harm's way. Anissa performed the combination proficiently enough that Richard asked, "Ready to go?" With that, Anissa put on headgear (which softens blows somewhat, though its primary purpose is to protect the face and ears from abrasions), a groin protector, and sparring gloves (which weigh more and are more heavily padded than gloves used in competition), stuck a mouthpiece between her lips, and climbed into the ring.

Anissa recalls:

I mostly sparred with Richard and Lori in those early days. It was really pretty overwhelming. I mean, it is hard to take when you first start sparring because it's something you've never done before. But I stuck it out. After a while, I started getting more and more into it. I began to relax more in the ring and I was able to do more. I remember one day when I'd been working really hard with Richard and Lori. We were taking turns in the ring, you know? Two of us at a time. I remember him asking me, "How many rounds do you think you've done?" He was kind of laughing when he said it. I was so caught up in it that I hadn't been keeping count. So I said, "I don't know. Three, I guess." He goes, "You've done seven." And I was like, Wow! But I knew then I could stick it out. I also started running a lot after I'd finished rehabbing my knee. We ran every day. There were a lot of women I started making friends with, and I was running with them. We'd meet at the Hike and Bike Trail on Town Lake and take off. We would run four, five, six, seven miles. It was so good.

Things happened for me really fast. I hadn't been at the gym for much more than about three months before I had my first fight, an amateur bout that took place at the La Zona Rosa nightclub in Austin. You know, I can't even remember who it was that I fought, it's been so long ago. To tell the truth, I don't even know if I won or lost. I just can't remember. It was just a brawl, a woman's brawl, nothing fancy. I didn't have much skill then and neither did the woman I fought.

You see, the first time you fight, it's just all like in your face all at once and you can't really remember anything. You're just too busy trying to cope with it. It's pretty fucking intense. To be honest with you, I wasn't sure if I wanted to do it again, I was like, Man, this is kinda crazy, you know?

It's way different from sparring. In sparring, you're working, you're training. In sparring, you're not trying to knock your opponent out. You're trying to learn. You're trying new things. In a fight, you're doing just that, fighting. It comes down to are you going to win or are you going to lose? It's you or her. She's trying to knock you out and you're trying to knock her out. The crowd is out for blood and wants to see someone on the ground. So basically you're making sure it's not you while doing everything you can to put her ass on the canvas. In sparring, you can kinda think about what you're going to do. But in a fight, your instincts pretty well take over. You can't take time to think about what you're going to do. By the time you've thought about what you're going to do, it's too late, you've missed your chance. That's why I say your instincts have to take over. What you do in the ring has to happen naturally. What I mean by that is you work on the fundamentals over and over and over until they become part of instinct. You just do them without thinking about doing them.

She did indeed win that first fight. A few weeks later, Anissa won another victory in the ring, but she still did not feel comfortable in the ring. In fact, this time she found boxing to be an overwhelming undertaking, even though she entered the ring with more skills and better conditioning than she possessed during her first fight. Her opponent was a firefighter from Houston, a strong woman who was in excellent shape. Anissa lost the first round, and she remembers retreating to the corner thinking, "Oh my God, what have I gotten myself into?" Richard calmly said to her, "Remember slipping?" Anissa said she did. Richard said, "Well, then, let's do something about it." And just like that, something clicked in her mind. She'd felt so overwhelmed by her opponent's skill and conditioning that she'd forgotten one of boxing's fundamentals: slipping punches. As a result, she'd taken a lot of hits. Focused, she went back into the ring and put her opponent down on the canvas twice for standing eight-counts by firing off basic one-two-three combinations, slipping, and counterpunching. The third round was more of the same as the firefighter from Houston ran out of steam and Anissa dropped her two more times to claim victory.

Anissa won her third amateur fight, this one a contest with a wrinkle. It was actually a kickboxing bout staged at the newly opened Austin Convention Center. Anissa's strategy was simple enough: She'd use a couple of kickboxing kicks she'd learned from her brother, then follow up with standard boxing tactics. It was a wild variant on how she'd been training to fight, but in the end it was a fun victory. This time she never felt overwhelmed in the ring.

. . . . .

It was at about this time that Richard Lord received a phone call from a man in Chicago who told him about a talented amateur boxer who recently relocated to Austin and who was ready to begin pursuing a professional career. Jesus Gabriel Sandoval Chavez had been born in Mexico but migrated to the United States with his family illegally when he was seven years old. Growing up in downtown Chicago, Chavez (then called Gabriel Sandoval) began boxing at ten years old. Idolizing the legendary Roberto Duran, Chavez ripped through the amateur ranks with a tenacity that would have pleased his rough-and-ready hero.

He might well have become one of Chicago's greatest professional pugilists had he not yielded to peer pressure at age seventeen and involved himself in a gang-related armed robbery. "One minute I've got my homework in my hand," he told Jan Reid years later, "and the next I'm robbing somebody? I threw away my friends. I threw away my family." Eventually apprehended by the police, he confessed and wound up serving three and a half years, most of it in the infamous state prison at Joliet, Illinois. Because he'd entered the United States illegally, albeit as a mere seven-year-old, and because he was now a convicted felon, the INS deported him, putting him on a plane for Mexico City as soon as he left prison.

Chavez remained in Mexico only a short while before returning to the United States and heading home to Chicago. But encounters with friends who were breaking the law in various ways persuaded him that he needed to find somewhere else to live. He chose Austin, a city he'd passed through on his return to Chicago, a city that had impressed him with its beauty, a city where he could connect with relatives who lived there, and a city where he might be able to revive his boxing career.

Not long after the phone call on his behalf was made, Chavez entered Richard Lord's gym for the first time. Chavez was not in fighting shape—far from it—but Richard knew he was the real thing as he watched Chavez work out. Richard and Chavez quickly reached an agreement: Richard would train and manage Chavez, first as an amateur, then as a pro. Chavez became one of a series of fighters who would actually live in Richard's gym while training. Of course, there was the matter of his illegal status. If he fought under the name Gabriel Sandoval he likely would be detected by the INS. So he would use a combination of his other two names, and from that time onward he has been known as Jesus Chavez, though some of his friends from his earliest days at the boxing gym still call him Gabe. In Chavez, Richard believed he'd found a fighter who could be a world champion, just as Curtis Cokes had been under the guidance of his father. Through the middle 1990s, Chavez and Anissa would be linked as Richard's marquee fighters. Moreover, Chavez would at times help train Anissa, spar with her, and often work in her corner during her fights.

Another male fighter who would be important to Anissa's career was Abel Davilla, a two-time Texas Golden Gloves champion. Davilla, who grew up in South Austin, fought as a welterweight (with a weight limit of 147 pounds), although his "walking around" weight between fights tended to balloon above that. He had been told by San Antonio cut man Joe Sousa that he would be fighting at the right weight class when he would be able to hit someone with all he had and the other guy wouldn't be able to get up. If the other guy was able to get up, he was in the wrong class. So welterweight it was for Davilla, even if it meant that losing a substantial amount of weight for a fight would be an excruciating part of his training regimen. Davilla acquired the reputation of being the master at "cutting weight" among the boxers at the gym.

In her early months at the gym, Anissa studied Davilla as he trained, impressed by how slipping, feinting, and counterpunching seemed to come to him so naturally. He had taken advantage of opportunities to learn the finer points of boxing when he'd sparred with the likes of champion boxers Jesse James Leija and Pernell "Sweet Pea" Whitaker. And when he fought, he brought that fundamental soundness into the ring. Many of the women Anissa saw in fights would start brawling as soon as the bell rang, forsaking the basics they practiced so diligently in the gym. Anissa wanted to be in control of herself when she fought, and Davilla stood as role model for how to do so. In addition to that, Abel would work the corner for some of Anissa's fights, as well as take a role in training her.

Late in Anissa's amateur career, a nonboxer who would have a significant impact on her career showed up at the gym. Still in his thirties, Richard Garriott was one of Austin's leading high-tech tycoons during the technology-crazed 1990s. The son of astronaut Owen Garriott, Richard was a self-taught programmer in the early 1980s who pioneered the development of fantasy computer games—indeed, he unveiled his first game, the landmark role-playing fantasy *Akalabeth*, when he was just nineteen years old. The money he made from *Akalabeth* allowed Garriott to attend the University of Texas in comfort. In the early 1980s, he developed the *Ultima* series of computer games and, eventually, with his brother and his father, created Origin Systems, one of the best-known and most influential companies in the history of computer gaming. *Ultima* has gone on to become the longest-running series of video games in history.

Famous in the gaming world, Garriott would further his reputation by building Britannia Manor, a fabulous estate famed in the early 1990s for being the home of the most elaborate Halloween haunted house in the United States, replete with dozens of actors and technicians. For visitors, it was like stepping into a fantasy game and becoming a part of it. People would fly into Austin and camp out in front of Garriott's house just to be part of it.

Garriott made his first visit to Richard Lord's gym after a mutual friend recommended it as an ideal place for him to get some exercise. Like many people who work out there, Garriott loved the gym ambiance, and he became an early morning fixture. But he wanted to be more than just some boxing dilettante; he wanted to become part of boxing, though he was too late in life to develop into an actual fighter. So Garriott eventually started working the corner during Anissa's fights.

One of the tasks a cornerman has is to hold the spit bucket to the fighter's mouth between rounds. It is perhaps an undignified act, but Garriott did it willingly. In fact, he would often wear a special jacket with SPITBOY stitched on the back while perform-ing his chores in the corner—a remarkable thing for a fighter like Anissa, having one of the wealthiest men in Texas work as her spitboy.

Beyond his duties in the ring, Garriott developed a friendship with Anissa, just as he had with Jesus Chavez. Garriott and his girlfriend frequently traveled to Anissa's out-of-town fights, even if he wasn't working the ring, and he took hundreds and hundreds of photographs of her in action.

Anissa was an amateur boxer for a short period before she turned pro: a little more than eighteen months, with just three fights. It might have lasted longer had not Richard received a phone call at the gym from a matchmaker seeking a female fighter who could take part in a pro bout with little notice because the boxer sched-uled for the fight had been forced to withdraw.

Yes, Richard answered, he did have someone.

With that, Anissa advanced to the pro ranks.

During her match with Brenda Rouse at the Grand Biloxi Casino on the Mississippi Gulf Coast, Richard Lord (right) gives Anissa between rounds fight instructions while her "spit boy," Richard Garriott, looks on from the lower left. (Photo Courtesy of Richard Garriott)

Anissa was most successful in the ring when she took the fight to her opponent, working inside, staying busy. (Photo Courtesy of Richard Garriott)

Anissa and Richard Lord enjoy a laugh during pre-fight preparations at a match at a Mississippi casino. Lord managed and trained Anissa throughout her professional career. (Photo Courtesy of Richard Garriott)

Most ringside fans at Anissa's fights had no idea that the "spit boy" on her team was Richard Garriott, one of Texas' wealthiest businessmen who built his fortune as a pioneer in the video game industry. Garriott, the son of NASA astronaut Owen Garriott, would go on to become the first son of an astronaut to travel in space in a highly publicized flight in 2008. (Photo Courtesy of Richard Garriott)

Two-time world champion boxer Jesus Chavez trained along Anissa at Richard Lord's Boxing Gym in Austin. Chavez worked Anissa's corner in her upset victory over Maribel Zurita for her second world championship. (Photo Courtesy of Richard Garriott)

Though Anissa won the fight, Brenda Rouse scores with a solid right cross to Anissa's chin in their August 1997 match. Rouse was managed by Tommy Morrison, who was famous for a heavyweight title he won in the early 1990s and for his claim of kinship to John Wayne. (Photo Courtesy of Richard Garriott)

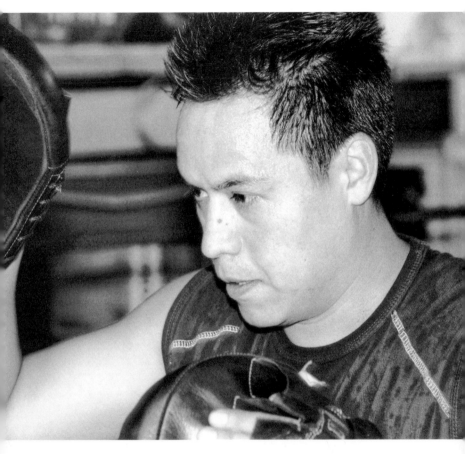

*In the second half of her career, Anissa benefited from her sessions with noted Mexico City boxing trainer Flaco Castrejon, who also helped guide Jesus Chavez to his two world championships. Castrejon eventually relocated from the Mexican capital to Georgetown, just outside Austin, and continues to train boxers.
(Photo Courtesy of Richard Garriott)*

"It hurts to box. People look at you and say, 'Well, you're in shape, you're ready to box.' It's more than that." —Anissa (Photo Courtesy of Richard Garriott)

*Both Anissa and Jolene Blackshear endured great suffering during their
1997 fight in Lula, Mississippi. At the end of the ten-round bloodfest, Blackshear
was declared the victor, but her win came at a terrible physical cost.
(Photos Courtesy of Richard Garriott)*

Abel Davilla, the master of cutting weight, was an important early influence in Anissa's career. He worked her corner during her pioneering professional debut in New York, and Anissa learned many of the fundamentals of her style by watching Abel while sparring at Richard Lord's Boxing Gym. (Photo Courtesy of Richard Garriott)

Anissa scores with a wicked overhead right in one of her early professional fights, crushing her opponent's nose. (Photo Courtesy of Richard Garriott)

Richard Lord promoted a popular series of fights at the Austin Music Hall under the billing of The Brawl in the Hall. Anissa fondly remembers the party-like atmosphere at the events. Without question, she was a crowd favorite whenever she entered the ring. Among those cheering the loudest were members of her family. Shown above, at the left, in dark T-shirts are her father and her stepmother.
(Photo Courtesy of Richard Garriott)

Anissa is at boxing peak in this publicity photo taken after her 1999 victory over Francesca Lupo for a WIBF world championship title. She's buff, flashing her trademark smile and sporting the champion's belt, but clearly visible on her shoulders are bite scars, souvenirs of her dark days at Brookhaven. (Photo Courtesy of Richard Lord)

Rockin' Melinda Robinson (right), an Austin police officer, was one of the first female fighters to train at Richard Lord's Boxing Gym. Here Anissa spars with Robinson in the ring at the gym. (Photo Courtesy of Richard Garriott)

Anissa is declared winner of her third fight against Maribel "Little Thunder"
Zurita in San Antonio. It was Anissa's final fight as a professional and it won her
a second world title—much to Zurita's dismay. (Photo Courtesy of Richard Lord)

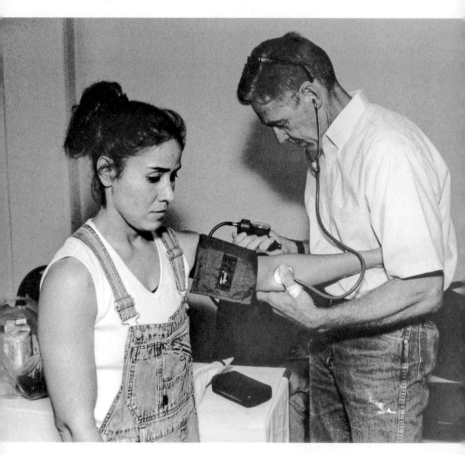

Anissa gets her blood pressure taken during the physcial examination that's a part of a prefight weigh-in. The weigh-in process ensures that both fighters are within the limits for their weight categories and that their vital signs are in the normal range. The physician examing Anissa is Jerry Baugh of Austin, who often served as the fight doctor at her bouts. (Photo Courtesy of Richard Lord)

Anissa is all smiles following a victory in the ring, but even wins can come at a price—in this case a blackened left eye. (Photo Courtesy of Richard Lord)

Jill "the Zion Lion" Matthews (right) squares off with Anissa at the Tropicana in Atlantic City in the second of their three-fight series. Each fighter was declared the winner of one fight in the series, with the second fight scored a draw, though Anissa contends she really won the fight. (Photo Courtesy of Richard Lord)

Lori Lord, Richard Lord, and Doug Lord (left to right, surrounding Anissa)
celebrate in the ring after Anissa wins one of her championships.
(Photo Courtesy of Richard Lord)

*Buffed, strong, and ready to rumble, Anissa poses in her boxing prime
for a publicity photo at Richard Lord's Boxing Gym.
(Photo Courtesy of Anissa Zamarron)*

The career of two-time world champion boxer Jesus Chavez (left) was intertwined with Anissa's as they fought out of Richard Lord's Boxing Gym in Austin. Chavez helped with Anissa's training, sparred with her, and sometimes worked her corner during fights, including her final one, when she won her own second world title. Richard Lord is on the right. (Photo Courtesy of Anissa Zamarron)

Anissa lands a hard right on Maribel Zurita's chin during what turned out to be Anissa's last pro fight. Anissa lifted hometown-favorite Zurita's world championship crown in a close decision. (Photo Courtesy of Anissa Zamarron)

Richard Lord (left) and Richard Garriott celebrate Anissa's second world title in San Antonio in 2005. (Photo Courtesy of Anissa Zamarron)

CHAPTER SIX

*On the one hand, the press was making a big deal out of this
being the first women's fight in New York. But at the same
time, they treated us—Andra and me—like we weren't really
important, like we were just some sort of weird sideshow or
something. You know what I mean?*

—ANISSA

. . . . .

Though it didn't register with her in historical terms at the
time, Anissa was playing a role in ensuring women's boxing
would be more than just a novelty when she boarded a plane for
New York in April 1995. Her pro debut hardly could have been a
more auspicious, perhaps even audacious, beginning. She took part
in the first-ever sanctioned professional boxing match for female
fighters in New York state.

New York has been the Mecca for boxing in America, and the
sport receives more press coverage there than anywhere else in the
nation. Anissa's initiation into professional boxing occurred at
the Huntington Hilton Hotel in the town of Melville on Long
Island, just thirty-five miles from New York City, the media capital
of the world. It's no surprise, then, that this first-of-its-kind event
attracted the interest of significant sports journalists like Robert
Lipsyte, who opined in the *New York Times,* "Tonight . . . Andra
Gorman, a Maryland nursery school teacher, will box Anissa
Zamarron. . . . It's a few rounds early to declare a trend beyond the
recent upsurge of upscale women aerobicizing through bloodless
sparring, but it's never too early to pontificate on gender matters.
Women's boxing may well be a freak show, but women boxers are

no freaks. Is it hypocritical for promoters to feature 'chorus girls' holding up the round cards during the men's bouts on the same card? Beats me. Call Don King or one of boxing's heavyweight ethicists. . . . But let the men worry. It's their matches that are in danger of being devalued."

More than a dozen years later, Richard Lord recalls sensing that the promoter in New York figured Anissa would be mere fodder for the evening's star, Gorman. After all, Anissa was merely one of the fifty or sixty amateur female boxers to be found in the United States at the time, an unknown from flyover country, while Gorman was an East Coast woman who'd already been heralded for her pioneering efforts in women's boxing. Anissa was such an unknown that Lipsyte erroneously referred to her as a Golden Gloves champ. He even got her hometown wrong, saying she came from San Antonio.

Gorman, on the other hand, was a bit of a sensation. She had been the subject of a feature in the Metro section of the *Washington Post* a year earlier, with good reason. A mother of three and a holder of a degree in fine arts from Hofstra University, she had been Maryland's first sanctioned female amateur boxer. Her background and lifestyle were about as far removed from the typical boxer's as one could imagine: "Gorman and her husband [an attorney] live in an airy four-bedroom home in North Potomac, where the walls are pink and the vases and abstract artwork on the walls are elegant," wrote the *Post*'s Kevin Sullivan. Before taking up boxing, Gorman had been captain of her college gymnastics team, and she'd also been a competitive bodybuilder, once bench-pressing 325 pounds, more than three times her body weight (102 pounds). In the early 1990s, she'd won a national kung fu championship for her weight class and had competed in tournaments in Taiwan and Europe. Then she'd taken up boxing, training under Charles M. Mooney Jr., an Olympic silver medalist on the 1976 American team. Gorman had already scored one win as a pro coming into her fight with Anissa. The downside for Gorman was that she was pushing forty years old that spring; Anissa was just twenty-four.

Because of another commitment, Richard could not travel to

New York to work Anissa's corner, so he sent Abel Davilla in his place. Difficult as it was for Anissa to face her first pro fight without her trainer and manager present, Abel was an apt substitute: Anissa had pounds to lose before the weigh-in, and she needed his direction to cut weight.

Anissa remembers, "I was weighing 112 or so and I had to get down to 106 by the weigh-in. Abel got me down there. The first couple of pounds came off real easy. But the day before the weigh-in, I still weighed too much. I just had a little bit of Gatorade that day, then hit the sauna and started sweating. It was tough, but by the next day, I was under 106. I mean, Abel knows how to do that. I think he could take twenty pounds off himself in a week if he needed to."

On top of that, she needed Abel to help her keep her head straight.

"I really didn't like traveling up there," she says, "because it was so different from what I was used to. I had to spend a whole week in New York City, and it was my first trip as a boxer. Really, it was about my first trip outside of Texas. There was so much press interest in that fight and it was overwhelming. I remember when the fight was over, I was ready to just go home and get away from there. I mean, I really didn't want to be there."

She and Andra sat in a hall prior to the start of their fight and it seemed to Anissa that everyone associated with the event was old school. One referee stopped by the check-in table in the hall to pick up his credentials for the night. He was a white-haired man and he announced loudly, "I refuse to do the women's fight! Don't put me down for it, don't assign it to me!"

Then he looked over and saw Anissa and Gorman. "No offense intended," he said sheepishly.

Anissa said, "I understand. It's not your deal."

The old man smiled and started to shuffle away. Anissa smiled too. But she was thinking: You know, all these old people, they gotta die soon, and once they're all dead, we can turn over a new leaf with fresh blood in their place. "So it was these old white guys up there who had issues," she says now. "The man who ended up officiating was Asian—I think he was Korean. I've seen him work fights on TV several times since then. He was cool with women fighting."

The evening crawled by until finally it was time for Anissa and Gorman to fight. Anissa was so new to prizefighting that she didn't know that for years boxers have made their way from the dressing rooms to the ring to musical accompaniment—ring entry music, sometimes called walk-up music. She arrived in Melville tuneless. That's okay, the promoters told her. We'll find something for you. When the doors opened for Anissa to make her entrance, the thundering bass of Janet Jackson's "Black Cat" shook the room. It was a song to which Anissa had no particular connection. But it worked for her. As she made her way down the aisle through the haze of cigar smoke, she began to get pumped up by the music and the cheers of the crowd. I can do this, I can do this, she heard something inside herself saying. *I can do this.*

Anissa climbed into the ring. Abel leaned down and stuck her mouthpiece on her teeth. "Now go out there and kill that fucking bitch!" he said. At the bell, Anissa hurried toward the center of the ring, her chin held high—"the absolute worst mistake a boxer can make." Gorman instantly picked up on Anissa's slipup and plugged her squarely on the tip of her chin. The blow was a hard one, hard enough to put a lot of fighters on the canvas. Anissa recalls, "That first time I got hit, it was a lot worse than what I experienced in amateur fights. You see, the gloves are smaller. The bigger the gloves, the less it hurts to get hit, and the less it hurts your hands to hit somebody else, because you have more padding. In the women's amateurs, we were fighting with ten-ounce gloves. But in the pros, it was eight-ounce gloves. Now, it may not sound like much, but that two-ounce difference changes a lot. Also, the gloves we use as pros are padded differently from the amateur gloves. And that makes hitting hurt more too." Though staggered and hurting, she somehow remained on her feet, realizing that this was no game, that she had to decide that very moment if she was going to bow down or if she was going to see the fight through to the end. Anissa could only choose the latter.

A different Anissa emerged from her corner for the second round. She took charge of the fight, discovering ways to evade Gorman's defenses and land blow after blow. In the third round, Anissa stunned Gorman with a shot that could have led to a knockout, but because of her inexperience, Anissa didn't know how to finish off her opponent. That allowed Gorman to survive the round and gave her a chance to recover in her corner. As the fight progressed, Anissa decided Gorman really wasn't any tougher than the amateur women she'd fought back home in Texas. That boosted her confidence. As did the exhortation she received from Abel: "Beat the shit out of her." The tough language may seem shocking outside the context of a boxing match, but Anissa was learning—very quickly—that "staying jacked up" for the duration of the fight was essential. Whoever stood across from her was going to be jacked up and ready to harm her if she had a chance. It was a fight, a fucking fight, not some game. Start messing around out there, and you easily wind up badly injured or dead. For the most part, if you have a bad day in baseball, you lose a game. Big deal. You'll do better tomorrow. Lose a boxing match and you're physically damaged, bruised, bleeding, in great pain.

"I knew I had her hurt several times during that fight," Anissa says, "and they had to give her a few standing eight counts as things went along. I totally dominated that match. To tell the truth, I just beat the crap out of her. It was a good old-fashioned ass-whipping." The judges agreed. They awarded her a unanimous decision.

. . . . .

Anissa returned to Austin a full-fledged prizefighter with a significant victory. She had impressed the boxing cognoscenti who'd seen her performance. One New York trainer had predicted to his fighter that someday Anissa could win a world championship. She'd also done well financially. A hundred dollars a round was a common rate paid to professional female boxers in those days, but Anissa received $2,500 plus expenses for her four rounds in

New York state's first sanctioned female boxing match, more than six times the going rate. Sure, Abel would get some of that as her cornerman and Richard would get a cut as her manager; still, she took home more than most female pros at that time. And she was in demand as a fighter.

Just six weeks later, Anissa returned to the East Coast for her second pro fight. This time the match took place at the Foxwoods Resort Casino on the Mashantucket Pequot reservation in Connecticut, just across Long Island Sound from where her first fight had occurred. Her opponent was thirty-one-year-old Jill Matthews, who billed herself as "the Zion Lion." With her flowing strawberry blonde hair, piercing eyes, high cheekbones, and sculpted abs, Matthews made a distinctive visual impression in the ring. She also displayed distinctive pugilistic skills in the ring. As an amateur, she had become the first woman in history to win a New York Golden Gloves title, defeating both her opponents in the tournament in the first round. One New York sportswriter observed that she "plain beat the hell" out of her opponents. With just her two amateur fights behind her, the Zion Lion, who trained out of the legendary Gleason's Gym in Brooklyn, was making her pro debut against Anissa.

White, Jewish (the daughter-in-law of a rabbi), and a college graduate with a husband who worked as a Park Avenue attorney, Matthews seemed at first glance to hail from an entirely different world from Anissa's. In fact, the two women shared a great deal. As a child, Matthews suffered from hyperactivity, which caused problems at school. She took up gymnastics as a way to burn up her excess energy. Though her family situation was not quite the same as Anissa's, Matthews did grow up under trying circumstances in tough urban areas. "My mother's name I can give you, and that's about it: Marilyn Matthews," she once told a reporter. "My father's name [was] different every week." Often she would be the only Jewish kid—as well as the only white child—in the neighborhood. She came out of adolescence feeling angry, alienated, depressed. She took up boxing as a young woman in part to offset those moods of hostility and despair. Like Anissa, she was fascinated with guitars and rock music, but Matthews pursued the fantasy: She fronted a punk band called Times Square. Matthews may have supported herself as a hairstylist, but when she spoke about boxing, she did so with the street-tough flair you might expect to hear from a longshoreman—or, for that matter, from Anissa. She told one writer: "They don't know I'll fight to the fucking death. If I bust someone up, do I enjoy it? Yeah. It's either me or her."

Before the fight, it seemed likely Anissa might be the one to get busted up. Anissa traveled to Connecticut nursing a bad cold. She had no difficulty making weight for the fight, but the cold sapped her energy in spite of the herbs she was taking to treat it. She spent all the day before the fight in bed. When the actual day of the fight rolled around, she hardly felt better. In fact, when it came time to dress for the bout, she was so listless that she didn't care much about how she'd look in the ring. She just pulled her trunks over the shorts she'd been sleeping in—"like something you'd see in an old movie, where some sick guy puts his suit on over his pajamas."

Anissa sleepwalked her way through the first round, allowing Matthews to win it without too much effort. The one positive thing about the round was that Anissa did hit Matthews above the eye, cutting her. But there was little else for Anissa to brag about during the round. As soon as Anissa landed on her stool for the rest period between rounds, Richard slapped her face a few times, shouting, "Wake up! Wake up! What the fuck are you doing? Look, I want you to go out there in the next round and put her on the fucking ropes, and I don't want you to let her off the ropes until they stop the fight!"

Anissa was grateful for those slaps. They indeed did lift her out of the fog. Digging deep into her resolve, she fought hard during the second round, following Richard's instructions. She pressed Matthews at every opportunity, forcing her against the ropes, striking her with uppercut after uppercut—and every chance she got, Anissa hit the cut that gaped ever larger above Matthews's eye until the referee stopped the fight and awarded Anissa a technical knockout.

Once the fight had been called, Anissa started to feel regret about the cut. She thought she should apologize or something, and—still a little woozy from the cold—she ambled over to Matthews's corner. "Hey," she said to the loser, "I'm sorry. Do you want to go get a drink or something?"

It was an unheard of thing to happen in boxing, a winner asking a loser out for a drink immediately after a fight. Matthews looked at Anissa in disbelief and said, "Get the fuck out of here."

Anissa left the ring, still feeling bad about the TKO. In years to come, she'd get over those feelings of remorse when she'd KO or TKO an opponent. But now she felt haunted by the knowledge that it could have been her with the bloodied face and the defeat on her record. You just never know how things might turn out.

Matthews had intended to box in one pro match after winning the Golden Gloves. But in losing to Anissa, Matthews found the inspiration to continue her own boxing career. She challenged herself to be able to fight competitively with boxers like Anissa and perhaps claim her own world title eventually. Anissa and Matthews wound up fighting three times in the 1990s, a rivalry that was important to both fighters' careers.

. . . . .

Anissa's next fight took place in her native Texas, and it presented her with some significant obstacles: It would be six rounds instead of four; she would be fighting a larger opponent (115 pounds; Anissa and Matthews had both fought at 108 pounds); and she would be facing a world champion in twenty-four-year-old Delia "Chikita" Gonzalez, who already had eight pro fights under her belt.

Gonzalez came from Chamberino, New Mexico, just across the state line from El Paso. Like Gorman and Matthews, Gonzalez had been a groundbreaking female boxer. As an eleven-year-old, she began training under her father, a onetime amateur boxer, at the San Juan Boxing Gym in El Paso. Her first day there, the gym had a sign on the door reading NO FEMALES ALLOWED.

The next day, the sign was gone. Thus, while still a little girl, she opened up that gym for women. But she would train for more than ten years before she finally had an opportunity to fight a woman for the first time. In order to get fights, Gonzalez had to keep her weight near 130 pounds; there simply weren't enough smaller women fighting professionally at lighter weights for her to stay busy. In those early fights, she usually appeared to be smaller than her opponents—hence, her nickname, "Chikita." Fighting on an all female card at the Aladdin Hotel in Las Vegas, Chikita had won the bantamweight title of the Women's International Boxing Federation (WIBF). Now she was prepared to defend that title against Anissa in Brownsville.

So Anissa had a lot on her mind as she left Austin for the Valley. Jesus Chavez was on the card as well, so a sizable entourage from Austin made the journey to Brownsville, including Doug Lord. At that point, Anissa didn't know Doug very well. But she took a liking to him as she got to know him during the trip. After spending some time with her, Doug realized that Anissa was having trouble controlling her nerves and staying focused on the upcoming title fight. He talked to her about it and eventually asked, "Would you like me to hypnotize you?"

Anissa wasn't sure at first. For her, the word "hypnotize" conjured up bad television sitcoms in which a nightclub hypnotist makes people behave like chickens or something along those lines. No, Doug assured her, it was nothing at all like that. He thought he could help her. Anissa agreed to give it a shot. Doug told her to write down some things she wanted to be sure to concentrate on during her fight—what kind of combinations she wanted to throw, for instance. Anissa made her list, then got back with Doug. The two of them retired to a quiet room, far away from ringing telephones, TVs, and loud conversations. Then Doug hypnotized her for the first time.

Whatever fear Anissa had about being turned into a chicken disappeared as Doug discussed the items on her list, then helped her to focus her thoughts on nothing at all. At that point, he told her to start relaxing, beginning at the top of her head. She began to feel whatever concerns she had flow away from her body as Doug's voice calmly instructed her to relax, relax, relax, moving from her head downward through her shoulders, then through her torso and legs, all the way down to the tips of her toes. Once her body was noodle-limp, her mind locked onto nothing at all, Doug began making suggestions based on the list she'd given him. Then he told her he wanted her to act on those suggestions whenever she heard him call out "Hustle!" to her during the fight. Finally, he led her back from the hypnotic state she'd been in. If nothing else, she felt calmer and more determined than she had for days.

She climbed between the ropes that night feeling relaxed and confident, even though Gonzalez was bigger and more experienced than she—and a world titlist to boot. Anissa was unsure of what to expect. She learned quickly that Chikita did not hit hard, at least not as hard as Richard or Jesus or the other guys she sparred with at the gym. Anissa went to her corner after the first round pumped up: "She can't hurt me!" she told Richard. "She doesn't hit hard!"

"I told you she can't be more than the guys you've been train- ing with," Richard said. He instructed her to charge into the next round and take care of business.

She tried, and Doug Lord's calls of "Hustle! Hustle! Hustle!" helped her remember to do what she wanted to accomplish, but in the end Gonzalez's experience was too much for Anissa to over- come. "She knew things I didn't know yet," Anissa says, "like how to tie up your opponent. She'd tie me up and I didn't know how to respond to that. She knew all the little tricks. She had a way of throwing her hooks that was different from anything I'd ever encountered. And she burned me with them."

Anissa came up short in her bid to take Gonzalez's title from her. In fact, Chikita won by unanimous decision. But once the announcer confirmed the decision, Richard said to her, "You may not have won, but you did really, really well."

Anissa took the loss about as well as anyone could. She says, "There are some fighters who take a loss and disappear. But there was no way that was going to happen to me. At this point in my career, I was just like a little sponge. I was soaking up whatever I could. Even after my first fight with Andra Gorman, it was like I knew what kind of fighter I wanted to be. It was like, Okay, that was my first fight, I got it out of the way, but I didn't look the way I wanted to look. It was too much of a catfight. You know what I'm saying? I was just in that mode. I wanted to get better and better and better. I knew I had the heart to be a good boxer. I just needed to get the skills. I lost to Delia, but I learned from it. I'd be able to use what I learned whenever I fought after that. So there was value in that fight, even if I lost."

She also decided that Doug Lord's hypnosis had helped her perform better. He frequently hypnotized her before future fights.

. . . . .

In August 1995, Richard initiated a series of hometown boxing matches to be held in the Austin Music Hall, a concert venue in a trendy area of downtown known as the Warehouse District. In the years to come, there would be between fifteen and twenty "Brawls in the Hall," each featuring star boxers from Richard's gym, with part of the proceeds going to charity. Rockin' Melinda Robinson, an Austin police officer who'd once fought Christy Martin, Jesus Chavez, and Anissa received top billing on the posters advertising the first Brawl in the Hall. In their pictures on the posters, Jesus and Anissa in particular look impossibly young, as if they were still carrying baby fat. But they both showed they were serious, experienced fighters that first hot summer night, with Jesus TKO-ing Mexico's Hector Vincencio and Anissa claiming a four-round unanimous decision over Tara Walsh of Lynchburg, Virginia.

Her appearances at the Brawl in the Hall were important for Anissa. In many ways Anissa remained the little girl who craved attention and recognition for her accomplishments, the little girl who wanted to be idolized like rock star Pat Benatar. The Brawl in the Hall salved that kind of desire. To Austin fight crowds, she became a celebrity. She received boisterous applause when she entered the ring at the Austin Music Hall, and her victories there elicited standing ovations. Her successes were reported in her hometown newspaper and she made appearances on TV and radio stations.

It's no surprise, then, that she entered a prolonged period when her demons were at bay. Boxing required her to adhere to a regimented life, with much of her days and nights consumed by physical training. She was eating nutritious meals. She eschewed hard drugs and other debilitating substance abuse, limiting herself to the occasional beer and the occasional hit off a joint while partying between fights—and toking weed eventually went away altogether. And she was achieving success in a sporting event that demands high levels of courage, discipline, and willpower. Because of the recognition of her achievements, she felt as if she was *somebody*. Emotionally, she was the healthiest she'd been since she was a very young girl living in San Angelo prior to her parents' divorce. On top of that, the Brawls in the Hall were a lot of fun.

Anissa remembers:

It was about this time that Richard had one of the very first T-shirts made up for me. You know, those T-shirts were to promote me as a boxer. This one was green, and it had my name on it, and there was a cyclone on the back. I made a comment to Richard about how not too long ago nobody wanted to have anything to do with me, but now they were all wanting to buy my T-shirt. That just felt so good. You know, my family, they didn't think I would ever amount to anything, they didn't want me around or anything—they probably didn't even think I'd still be alive at this point—but now they were buying my T-shirt too. Roland started taking care of me on the day of fights. If the fight was here in town, I'd stay over at his place so no one could bother me. I'd get a lot of rest there. Then he'd be the one to take me to the fight. My brother Ramon came to some of the fights. Most of the time, my mom would be there. My dad came too. I even had a half-sister from San Antonio— she was my dad's daughter from a marriage before he married my mother—she came to some too.

It was kind of weird, thinking back on it. The only time when my family really all got together would be at one of my fights in Austin. When I went for stretches when I wasn't fighting, we wouldn't see each other.

Another weird thing: Back when I was a screwed-up kid, and I was dreaming about playing the guitar and being a rock star and all that, I had a school counselor who was a part-time artist. This counselor made me this poster thing that showed me as a rock star—it's real cool, me playing the guitar, and I still have it. Well, it actually turned out to be sort of an omen. I did end up with my picture on a poster, but instead of a concert poster, it was a fight poster.

When I was in therapy, the psychologist once said, "The only reason you want to be a rock star so badly is so that your family will pay attention to you." That comment sticks in my mind. I guess it is kind of true. By becoming a fighter, my family started paying attention to me. And I'd bring them all together, not at a concert, but at a fight. Maybe that was always playing in the back of my mind, bringing everyone back together, trying to keep them together.

CHAPTER SEVEN

*But then it all settles in around you: You lost. I mean, that
day you came back, you felt good because everyone was telling
you that you really won, that you got robbed. And you're still
all pumped with adrenaline and it's great. But then, the next
morning when you wake up, you have to face it: You lost and
you're like a deflating balloon or something. It's a loss.*

—ANISSA

. . . . .

Her first Brawl in the Hall might have been fun and earned
her hometown accolades, but Anissa had little time to rest
after demolishing Tara Walsh. Less than two months later, she
was back on the East Coast, facing Andra Gorman once more.
Again, Anissa proved to be too much for the older fighter, winning the four-round rematch decision unanimously. Less than six
weeks after the Gorman fight, Anissa boarded an intercontinental
flight. Her destination: Germany. Her opponent: one of the greatest champions women's boxing has known.

Regina Halmich was just nineteen years old in December
1995, but she already was an experienced boxer—she turned pro
at seventeen, after quitting her job as a law clerk—with a stellar
record. She'd fought thirteen pro fights, losing just once, and she
held the WIBF's junior flyweight title. She and Anissa were scheduled to battle for ten rounds, with Halmich's WIBF title on the
line. It would be a landmark event for Anissa, her first ten-round
fight. Eventually she'd be credited by some followers of the sport
with having fought more ten-round fights than any female boxer
in history.

The fight was scheduled to take place in Karlsruhe, Germany, which is in the southwestern part of the country, near the French border. It is the city where Halmich was born on November 22, 1976. If traveling to New York City for her first pro fight caused Anissa discomfort, flying halfway around the world to Karlsruhe was flat out scary. She had to hustle around to get a passport, then jump a plane for Germany. Unsure of what she'd face in terms of food there, Anissa took a supply of peanut butter and jelly with her, as well as tortilla chips and salsa, just as any good Texas girl would. Once on the ground, she fought jet lag for the first time in her life.

That the fight would be televised all over Europe intimidated her. She had been on television before—her first-ever professional bout in New York wound up on TV—but her upcoming fight in Karlsruhe was being treated as a big deal by the European television producers. When she checked out the ring for the first time, she was surprised by how many TV lights had been installed. She knew that meant the ring would be extremely hot, and she was glad she'd done all that training in the summer and fall heat at Memorial Stadium back in Austin. The ring appeared to be just about new. She'd learned that even in high-profile fights back in the States, the rings seemed to be shoddy, as if they were held together with nothing more than duct tape and baling wire. She stepped out onto the clean, tight canvas and bounced a little, shifting her weight from one foot to the other. Everything felt solid. As she climbed through the ropes, she noticed they were extremely tight—again, a major improvement over what she was used to back home. So the ring itself would be a benefit.

As the opening round of the fight grew closer and closer, Anissa worried about the length of the bout. Ten rounds required a lot of stamina. Even with all the conditioning she'd put herself through, she was uncertain if she could go the distance. After all, ten rounds of boxing a top-rank opponent sucked much more out of you than even running stadium stairs in July.

When Anissa entered the ring for the preliminaries, she quickly discovered her concerns about the heat from the TV lights were well founded. It was so hot in the ring that the ice in the corner-men's buckets already was melting. But whatever concerns she had about going the distance with Halmich also melted as the first round progressed. After the bell rang to end it, she came back to the corner feeling confident. "I was sort of like, Do-do-do-dee-do-do-do, this isn't so bad," she remembers.

Halmich fought as if she wasn't really ready for the fight Anissa presented her that night: one speed, full-out, like a freight train. "I was throwing a million punches around," Anissa says. "I was like, Let's get this show on the road!" Halmich had come from a kickboxing background, and like a lot of martial artists who take up boxing she stood up too straight, making herself vulnerable to those million punches. Anissa was confident she was scoring heavily.

Anissa fought energetically through the first four rounds. But after the fifth, she came back to her corner feeling fatigued. Richard had warned her this would be coming. She was entering into what he told her was known as "the deep water," the time to sink or swim, and if you opted to sink, you drown. The deep water is the measure of a championship-caliber fighter, finding some force deep down that keeps her going, throwing punches, slipping, feinting even though she feels like she doesn't have the strength to do it. The water only gets deeper with each passing round. By the end of the seventh round, Anissa was pleading with herself: Oh my God, what am I going to do?

Between the eighth and ninth rounds, Richard said, "Look, it's like you have a simple little three-round amateur fight left to go. Just suck it up and do it!" It was easy enough for him to say, but Anissa felt like she'd just smacked into a cement block wall—and smacked it hard. Still, she managed to finish the fight. She was sure Halmich had struggled in the deep water as much as she had. As the judges tallied their scorecards, Anissa felt confident she'd won. But she was about to learn a hard lesson about the world of boxing. She says, "Now I want you to understand, I like to be honest about how I perform when I box. When I fought Delia Gonzalez, I lost. She beat me. No question about it. I own up to that. But to tell the truth, I beat Regina that night in Germany. I won that fight hands down. The crowd and the referee, they were like they knew I won that fight. The referee, he was from Austria, right next door to Germany, and you'd think because of that he'd be favoring Regina, but he said to me, 'You won that fight.' I got tanked because it was her show in her hometown, with her judges."

Reporters jumped into the ring to interview Halmich. Though Anissa spoke not a word of German, she could tell by Halmich's tone of voice that she was being defensive. Anissa decided Halmich knew deep down that she'd lost the fight. Later that night, Anissa went to an after-fight party and the predominantly German crowd there gave her an enthusiastic standing ovation as she entered the room. When Halmich arrived a short time after Anissa, she received just polite applause. "Those Germans knew I'd been hosed," says Anissa.

Anissa's family greeted her with flowers at the Austin airport after she got off the return flight from Germany. The whole bunch of them went to Chuy's on Barton Springs Road for beers and Mexican food, and it was a nice outing. Her family assured her they all knew she'd really won and that made her feel good. But when she was alone she struggled emotionally with what had happened to her. She'd had something stolen from her, and she didn't like it.

. . . . .

Anissa did not fight again for four months, in part because there weren't a lot of fights available for her at that time, but also because she went on a serious streak of partying as she coped with what happened in Germany. When she returned to fighting, she rebounded with ferocity, destroying two lesser fighters, Stephanie Poole and Mireya Contreras, with first-round technical knockouts in fights a month apart. She'd quit her job at Abbott Laboratories after the company balked at giving her the time off she requested to train for and take part in the Halmich fight. So now her focus was on boxing full-time. She'd befriended a social worker named

Lynne* who trained at the gym, and to save on expenses, Anissa was renting a spare room from Lynne and her husband. Given the quality of her performance against Halmich and her two subsequent victories, Anissa seemed poised to make her mark as one of the finest female boxers in America.

But Anissa was about to enter a troubled phase of her life, one that threatened to derail her career. She'd fought Stephanie Poole in Dallas, and almost as if they were a harbinger of the difficulties to come in the next few months, Dr. Hellman, along with a former Brookhaven psychiatric nurse and a former patient, came to the fight. At the time, Anissa found it exciting that she was able to perform so well in Dallas before people with connections to the psychiatric hospital where she'd suffered through so much hell. Still, they served as a reminder of those dark times. In Austin, there were other reminders as well. Lynne's marriage was ending, and the strife that inevitably accompanies impending divorce was all too present in the house that Anissa was now calling home.

At the boxing gym, Anissa befriended a white-collar guy named Nelson* who had begun working out there to get in shape. Their friendship blossomed into romance, and Anissa unintentionally became pregnant. Given the circumstances she and Nelson were in at the time, Anissa saw no other alternative but to abort the fetus. Going through the process, however, was emotionally devastating for her. Making things worse was Nelson's reaction. "I mean," Anissa says, "it wasn't like I expected him to marry me or anything like that. I just expected that—well, we got each other in this bind, let's just stick it out for a few weeks, support each other, and maybe end up as friends. I thought he could have stuck with me for a while, at least hang out with me for at least a week or two until I could get my head back together a little bit. But he wigged out and broke up with me. He made himself sick, ended up in therapy, and I wound up leaving Austin for a while—I went back to San Angelo for a few weeks to heal up."

Eventually she and Nelson would become friends again, though not lovers. She didn't tell very many people about what all she'd been through. Richard had to know, of course. He had to cancel her appearance on a fight card. But while she was staying with her brother in San Angelo, she started working out again. And then when she returned to Austin, she started training in earnest, doing her best to leave Nelson alone, both in terms of physical contact and in her mind. Anissa just wanted to box.

. . . . .

As one might expect, the tumult surrounding the abortion took its toll on Anissa's boxing. She lost her next two fights, both to Christine Sullivan, an Austin boxer who trained at Richard Lord's Boxing Gym. Sullivan did not come close to possessing the fighting skills and experience of Anissa, so the losses came as a surprise to people following Anissa's career, people who didn't know what she'd just gone through with the abortion. And there was more to the story. Anissa had heard other women boxers disparage Sullivan's boxing skills behind her back. Hearing people saying those sorts of things bothered Anissa, resurrecting feelings she'd had in her life when she believed she was both unloved and unlovable. She understood what it was like not to be popular, to know people were talking behind her back. Anissa thought, If it's a big deal to her to win a fight, let her win. As a result, Anissa gave two of the most lackluster performances of her career when she fought and lost to Sullivan in Houston and then a month later at a casino in Kenner, Louisiana.

There was not enough of a break between that fight and her next outing for Anissa to regroup. A mere four weeks after her loss in Kenner, she traveled to Pharr in the Rio Grande Valley of Texas for a rematch with the always tough Delia Gonzalez. Before the knowledgeable and enthusiastic fight fans from the Valley, Delia gave an impressive display of the skills that made her a terrific champion. Anissa went down to defeat.

Anissa didn't fight for the next five months. But when she came back in January 1997, she did so with a vengeance. At a Brawl in the Hall, she faced Patty Stickler, who was fighting in her debut as a pro. Before Anissa could really work up a sweat in the first round, she sent Stickler tumbling to the canvas—"Oh, yeah, I really clocked her."

Unfortunately for Anissa, she had little time to savor the victory. Next up was Eva "Sweet Magic" Jones-Young from South Bend, Indiana. She was a half dozen years older than Anissa, but she was in the early stages of her boxing career, having fought only two previous fights. Her record was one win and one draw. But her novice status as a boxer belied her experience in fighting. She had claimed several national titles in karate and had achieved a black belt in tae kwon do. She'd also been undefeated in two bouts as a kickboxer. Moreover, Jones-Young was a left-handed fighter, and southpaws always present problems for right-handed boxers like Anissa. Finally, Anissa remembers her opponent as being much bigger than she—Jones-Young normally fought at 122 pounds but had come down in weight to fight Anissa. "I felt like I was going up against the Jolly Green Giant or something," Anissa says. Still, at the Brawl in the Hall in March, Anissa was favored to win.

As Anissa stepped into the ring, she felt a pop in her ankle followed by a "squishy" sensation. She realized she had injured herself in some way, but she saw Jones-Young in the corner opposite her and felt the pump of adrenaline she always experienced when fighting before the hometown fans at a Brawl in the Hall. She told herself she couldn't think about her ankle; she had to focus on fighting.

Sweet Magic proved to be a hard-hitting, aggressive boxer, one of the best Anissa would ever meet in the ring—Jones-Young eventually would become a world champion. On top of that, Anissa had grown used to fighting longer fights; this match was just four rounds. Jones-Young's left-handed skills, the short fight, the injured ankle—it all became too much for Anissa. For the first time in her career, she was knocked down. She recovered before the count was through and finished the fight; in fact, Anissa believes she came back to win the fourth round. But the damage was done. Jones-Young got the upset win. Says Anissa, "She was so hungry. I really got banged up in that fight." To make matters worse, her ankle injury from just before the fight never really improved. She'd cope with ankle and related knee problems for years before finally getting surgery.

Anissa now had lost four of her last five fights. Not surprisingly, retirement crossed her mind. At the very least, she thought she needed a break. Her friends from the boxing gym agreed with her, especially Lori Lord. Anissa had a hard time deciding just what she should do as rumors of her impending retirement spread through the gym. It bothered her that people were talking about it. After all, it was she who knew deep down what she was capable of, not them. But at the same time she knew their concern was well intentioned.

She needed someone to talk to, someone removed from the boxing gym yet someone who could appreciate the dilemmas she faced as a female athlete at that point in her career. She found an empathetic listener in Georgia Shaw, a martial artist and competitive cyclist who was also a massage therapist. They first got to know each other when Anissa began receiving massages from Shaw, but their client-therapist relationship soon developed into friendship. During their conversations, Anissa was able to sort out all she faced. In the end, she did take some time off, but then she gradually got back into training. Within a few months, she had a fight scheduled at a casino in Biloxi, Mississippi. This fight was sanctioned by a new women's boxing group, the International Female Boxers Association (IFBA). Anissa was determined to prove she was not washed up.

Her opponent, Brenda Rouse, hailed from Bartlesville, Oklahoma, a small city north of Tulsa that has thrived over the years on the petroleum industry. She was managed by fellow Oklahoman Tommy Morrison, himself a onetime World Boxing Organization heavyweight titleholder who had been lauded during his career for his hard punches, as well as derided for his weak chin. Morrison was a distant relative (designated "grandnephew") of movie icon John Wayne, whose real name was Marion Morrison. Tommy Morrison even appropriated Wayne's famous nickname, the Duke. And he followed his "granduncle" into acting, appearing in Sylvester Stallone's *Rocky V.* Just a year before Anissa's fight with

Rouse, Morrison's career abruptly came to a halt after a mandatory prefight blood test showed him as being infected with HIV, which disqualified him from boxing, although other blood tests conducted over the years following the initial one have shown him to be HIV-free. But Morrison was still under the cloud of the first blood test and was not fighting when he brought Rouse to Biloxi to box Anissa. Still, he was famous from his boxing days, and his fame brought a lot of attention to Rouse, who came into the fight favored over Anissa.

That night's card, featuring all female fighters, was broadcast on TV, and viewers were treated to an amazing performance from Anissa and Rouse. They went eight rounds virtually toe-to-toe, with Anissa the aggressor and Rouse counterpunching her. For the first half of the fight, Anissa kept Rouse against the ropes much of the time, winning the first four rounds. "Keep it up," Richard told her between rounds. "Keep her on the ropes. Don't let her breathe!" During the last four rounds, Rouse became more mobile, and it helped her with the judges, though Anissa remained the aggressor. The scorecards showed Rouse winning some of the last four rounds. But Anissa came back to dominate the last round, and she was awarded a unanimous decision in one of the finest performances of her career. In fact, she considered that fight to be a kind of coming out party, letting the boxing world see just what she was capable of.

Says Anissa, "Brenda was a damned good boxer. She worked hard, you know. She was one of the girls I faced where I was thinking, Holy shit, if I stand here and let her do it, this bitch can knock me out. She was that strong. Every time she hit me I saw flashes and stuff. But one thing I figured out early on is that she had a hard time fighting if you were moving her backward. So I found ways to keep backing her into the ropes. I remember telling myself over and over not to leave anything in the ring. That is, I had to leave that fight without a single regret. 'No regrets!' That was my slogan, and I kept repeating it to myself. I remember so well having her on the ropes and feeling so fucking tired, and everything inside me is telling me I need to back off, stop punching, rest, but I kept thinking, I'm not going to wake up tomorrow feeling sorry that I didn't find a way to keep pushing myself. So, to tell the truth, I ended up fighting my heart out. So it became a turning point for me, that fight with Brenda. I learned I could turn myself around mentally if I worked at it hard enough."

Anissa had resuscitated her career with her impressive win over Rouse before a television audience. Physically and emotionally she seemed fit for another victory in an IFBA-sanctioned fight, and two months later, she fought Jolene Blackshear at another Mississippi casino, this one the Lady Luck in the small town of Lula, not far south of Memphis.

Compared to Anissa, Blackshear was a ring novice with only one fight on her record. That spring, she had fought Yvonne Trevino in California. Trevino had been heavily favored, but Blackshear knocked her down twice in the first round, although the referee ruled them slips. Later in the round, Trevino struck Blackshear in the eye with her elbow, cutting her deeply. The fight was stopped in Trevino's favor over howls of protest, not just from Blackshear's corner but Trevino's as well. And the crowd shouted, "Bullshit! Bullshit! Bullshit!" as the decision was announced. Roughly the same age as Anissa, Blackshear was a short woman, standing only 4′11″, giving away a height and reach advantage to Anissa. But Blackshear was a skilled athlete in superb condition. She graduated from Sonoma State University with a degree in biology, and while in college she achieved All-Conference status for fast-pitch softball skills. She also competed on the varsity track and field team.

As Anissa entered the ring, she saw a short woman with rippled muscles across from her, but she didn't know much else about her—she certainly had no idea of what to expect from her as a fighter facing ten rounds of boxing. As it turned out, Anissa found herself fighting someone who in terms of style and ability was almost a duplicate of herself: "tough, one speed, straightforward, aggressive, very strong-willed." Pumped by her victory over Rouse, Anissa had trained hard for this fight too. But so had Blackshear. As soon as they began exchanging blows, Anissa knew she was going to be in for a tough night. Boxing reporter Erik Anderson wrote: "These two women poured everything into this fight and went at each other the whole way. Zamarron and Blackshear practically ran out of their corners to meet each other at the opening bell. They spent little time on the outside, preferring instead to stand toe-to-toe and throw bombs."

Anissa was beginning to dominate the fight in the second round when she backed Blackshear to the ropes with fierce left-right combinations, but Blackshear responded with a blow that broke Anissa's nose and began a blood torrent. For the next eight rounds, Anissa bled all over everything—the canvas, the ropes, Blackshear, herself. Blackshear suffered her own damage as well. By the end of the third round, her eyes were swollen and she had small cuts on her lips. Even with her broken nose, Anissa was the aggressor through much of the fight, with Blackshear withstanding her punishment, then finding an opening to hurt Anissa. At one point, she doubled Anissa over with a body punch, but Anissa remained on her feet. In fact, there were no knockdowns in the fight. When the tenth round was over, the two fighters hugged in the middle of the ring, both of them soaked in Anissa's blood, then waited for the decision.

Blackshear won the fight with a unanimous decision. In doing so, she claimed the vacant IFBA flyweight world championship. Although she lost, Anissa shared with Blackshear a roaring standing ovation for their performance. The match contributed to Anissa's reputation as a game boxer who would not let down the audience who'd paid to see her fight.

. . . . .

Two months later, in January 1998, Anissa hit the big time in terms of boxing venues in the United States. She traveled to Atlantic City for a rematch with Jill Matthews at the Tropicana Hotel and Casino. Atlantic City had been the frequent host of Mike Tyson's fights in the 1980s and '90s, so at the time it challenged Las Vegas and New York as the premiere showcase for professional boxing. There was plenty of glitz in the city once mostly known for its boardwalk and the Miss America pageant. An outstanding ring performance there would garner Anissa a lot of media attention.

Matthews's boxing skills had improved considerably since the two women's previous fight nearly two and a half years earlier. She'd fought five times, winning four of those fights. Her single loss had been in Denmark, where there had been a misunderstanding concerning which day the fight would occur and she went into the ring suffering from a sleep deficit. Her last two fights had ended with a TKO and a knockout, both coming in the first round. So the Zion Lion was much more dangerous now than she had been in 1995.

Media reports say Anissa predicted a second-round knockout, and she went into the fight brimming with confidence. She knew that the Jill Matthews she'd boxed in 1995 was not nearly as good as Jolene Blackshear. So she was certain she would win. But there would be no second-round knockout. The fight, with the vacant International Women's Boxing Federation's (IWBF) junior flyweight title on the line, went the full ten rounds, and the action was wide-open, nonstop, thrilling the crowd. In the end, the judges ruled the fight a draw. Legendary football coach Darrell K Royal once famously described a tie as being as rewarding as kissing your sister. For Anissa, it was much worse than even that. She was certain then that she had won the fight. "I thought I'd been robbed in Germany when I fought Regina," Anissa says, "and I thought I was robbed that night in Atlantic City. You know what I mean? I was thinking, What's the point if they're not going to let you have the victory when you've won the fight?"

Shortly after Anissa returned to Austin, her phone rang. Richard was on the other end. "Hey," he said, "guess what? Everybody's fighting for your fight."

"Huh?" Anissa said.

"You and Jill put on quite a show," Richard said. "A lot of people are interested in your rematch."

"I don't know," Anissa said. She was still feeling a little dazed after the draw decision. She wasn't in much of a mood to think about a rematch with Matthews.

"Well, do you want to do it?" Richard said, sounding frustrated.

"Hey, this is a great thing! I thought you'd be kind of excited about it."

Then he told her the interest in the rematch went beyond the United States. There were people talking about getting the money together to stage it as far away as South Africa.

But Anissa couldn't muster much enthusiasm about fighting Matthews again. Yet, in the end, she told Richard to arrange the rematch. Once all the talks concluded, the decision was that Atlantic City would host the rematch. Once again, Anissa and Jill would fight at the Tropicana. But the stakes would be greater for the rematch, for the winner would be both the IWBF and IFBA junior flyweight world champion.

Anissa arrived in Atlantic City with her mind in a bad place. The first time she fought there, it had been exciting to be chauffeured around in limousines. This time, it was not exciting at all. In fact, it intimidated her. Looking out the limo windows, she saw electronic billboards advertising ZAMARRON-MATTHEWS with pictures of both fighters. It scared her to see her name listed first — "like everybody expects you to win and there are no excuses if you don't." It was as if the whole world had become aware of her and watched to see what she would do. Anissa found herself feeling like a little girl from San Angelo who suddenly was in the Big City on the East Coast where people were waiting for a chance to chew her up and spit her out. Making matters worse, that old demon that had been sleeping inside her came awake and began to assert himself: You ain't nothing, you don't deserve to be here, you sure as hell don't deserve to win — all you deserve is to lose!

Says Anissa, "When it came time to fight, I just gave up. My heart wasn't in it and I talked myself out of the win. I was like, Fuck it, I don't give a fuck. That night that kind of attitude cost me two world titles."

By the end of the tenth round, Anissa appeared to some at ringside to be out on her feet. And it was Matthews who took home the two world titles.

Anissa reacted to the loss to Matthews by training lackadaisically for her next fight, set for June 14, 1998, once more in Atlantic

City. This time she took a step up in venues: She was on a card at the Trump Taj Mahal Hotel Casino. Her opponent was Patty "Ironheart" Martinez, a twenty-six-year-old native Californian who'd relocated to North Miami, Florida, where she worked as a court reporter. The previous year, Martinez scorched her way through the USA Boxing national amateur championship tournament, including an impressive win over Yvonne Caples. Her sack-and-burn campaign continued into the pro ranks. She dominated her first three pro fights; her opponents had a difficult time coping with her deft left-right combinations. One of the boxers she fought along the way was Brenda Rouse, over whom she won a unanimous decision.

Again, disaster seemed to loom for Anissa in Atlantic City. Martinez posed a dangerous threat, and Anissa prepared for the fight almost as if it were already lost. She arrived back in Atlantic City feeling burnt out, tired, not really caring about boxing anymore. One thing she did have going for her the night of the fight: There was no pressure on her at all.

Anissa remembers:

> So the fight starts and she comes out of her corner like a freakin'
> I don't know what. She was like banging on me nonstop and I
> was like, Shit! What's up with this bitch? She was aggressive,
> but aggressive like an amateur, you know? Like she didn't know
> how to pace a fight, especially over six rounds. So I just did what
> I had to do to keep up with her. Sure enough, probably around
> the middle of the second round, she ran out of gas.
>
> It dawned on me that I would have four and a half rounds
> with her at a disadvantage because she didn't have very much
> left. I took control and started beating her up. I know I gave her
> at least one standing eight-count. I read an account of the fight
> that said I hit her with a steady stream of lefts and rights. Well,
> yeah, I guess you might say that. I just felt stronger and stronger
> with every round.
>
> In the end, I saw the tally: I threw 546 punches over six
> rounds—almost 100 per round. Seventy-four percent of them

landed. Now, she was fucked because she threw too much in the first round, but that's not to say she wasn't still fighting. I think the count showed she threw around 75 or so fewer punches than I did over the six rounds. So she was staying as busy as she could. But you see, when you're tired like that, you're throwing wild punches, and I was able to avoid them. And because she was so wild, I was able to just pound away at her head. And I swear to God I was stronger at the end of the fight than I had been at the start.

It was a terrific victory for me. She was a good boxer, and I just handed her the first defeat of her career. I mean, later on down the line, she'd beat Maribel Zurita and a bunch of other good boxers. But I totally dominated her for a unanimous decision.

After that fight, Richard was like, "Okay, now you can retire, if that's what you want to do. You can end your career on this good note."

Like I said, the notion of me retiring had been brought up before. And I think Richard was trying to give me an out, if I wanted one. You see, it's not good for a fighter to keep fighting after she's used up or her head's not in it anymore. That's how you get in trouble, how you get hurt in a very bad way. But I decided to keep at it. At that point, my pro record was 8-9-1, and I didn't want to go out with a losing record. Especially since I knew some of those fights were ones I should have won—would have won if my head had been right. And a couple of those losses were outright robberies.

Well, it ended up that I didn't retire. Man, things would have been real different if I had quit then.

. . . . .

A month later, the question of retirement settled, Anissa fought Natasha Wilburn of Atlanta in a Brawl in the Hall in Austin. The fight provided Anissa with a payday and the opportunity to bring her record up to 9-9-1. And she completely outclassed Wilburn, who in seven previous outings had yet to win or even draw. All Wilburn could attempt to do was tie up Anissa with clinches.

Her next opponent would be no journeyman clincher like Wilburn, not by a long shot. In late September she and Doug Lord boarded a transatlantic flight for Germany, where she would challenge Regina Halmich at the Prinz-Garden-Halle in Augsburg for the WIBF world flyweight title she held. This time the fight took on a different complexion from their first one. And it was not to Anissa's advantage.

For reasons that perplexed her, Anissa discovered her attitude had reverted back to the negative place it had been before the Patty Martinez fight. Here she was, thousands of miles away from home and feeling uncertain about herself, and her manager and trainer was in another country: Jesus Chavez had a fight that conflicted with Anissa's rematch with Halmich, and Richard had traveled with Jesus instead of going to Germany with Anissa. She'd come to hold a great deal of affection for Doug Lord, who subbed for Richard in Augsburg, but it still wasn't like having Richard there.

Says Anissa: "I'm not sure that Richard fully understood at that point what all I had struggled with mentally and emotionally in my life. I know he knew I'd been through some stuff. But you see, he's not the kind of guy you sit down and tell all of those things to. I just never felt comfortable in telling him all that. And beyond everything I'd been through, I'm not sure I myself understood what it was that would affect me so bad at some times in my life. I think if I'd tried to tell him, it would have just frustrated him because he wouldn't have understood it. When I fought Regina for the second time, my head was at this place where I just wanted to be by myself all the time. I didn't know why, but that's how it was. I wanted to be alone. Now, I knew I had it in me to be one of the best fighters out there, and even when my head wasn't right, it would take a lot for somebody to be able to beat me. But I just didn't have the confidence or self-esteem or whatever to put it all together fight after fight, month after month, year after year. Like I said, Richard didn't know all that was going on inside me. On the other hand, he had a way of getting my head straight. Doug did his best to keep up with me that week, but Richard is the one who could have made me think right, and I didn't have him there."

If Anissa felt robbed after her first fight with Halmich, this time she knew the German champion had beaten her fair-and-square. Anissa suffered a broken finger in the second round, which made throwing punches painful. Worse, she took a number of shots to the head. Anissa flew back to the United States with her finger in a splint, her body and face bruised, her head swollen, and another loss on her record.

As often happened in Anissa's career, a deep low point occurred just prior to a dizzying high. Physically and emotionally battered, Anissa retreated to Austin to recuperate over the next four months. She had a losing career record once again. But during this bleak period, Richard managed to make a deal that would allow Anissa to fight for a world championship once more. She and Regina had fought at 108 pounds for the WIBF world flyweight title. Regina held on to that crown, but the WIBF's junior flyweight (104 pounds) world title was vacant. Richard made a match for Anissa to meet Italy's Francesca Lupo for that championship. Moreover, this title fight would take place as part of the Brawl in the Hall series. Anissa would have familiar surroundings and wildly enthusiastic friends and family there to support her.

Lupo came to fight, no question about it. Anissa won the first round, but then Lupo took charge of the fight. At one point between rounds, Richard said to Anissa, "You need to get busy! You're losing the fucking fight. You ready to get busy with her?"

The message clicked with her. "I thought, I can't lose this!" Anissa says. "Here I was, at home, with all these people cheering for me, and I had a chance to become world champion. I just couldn't lose this fight! The thing about it is, I just don't kind of give a fuck a lot of the time. I get myself in these 'Yeah, yeah, whatever . . .' states of mind, and somebody has to snap me out of it. When someone does that, I go, Oh fuck, okay! But when it doesn't happen, you know, I don't really realize until the next day just how fucked up I was. It's those freaking little demons in you that tell you that you aren't worth a shit, that nothing matters. They try to sabotage you into thinking that no one cares about you or anything you do, so fuck it. But then, the next day, you say, What the fuck did I do? So with Francesca, it almost came to that point. I almost let it slip away. They had to snap it out of me to get busy and to win it after I started going into a lull in those early rounds. It is really strange how that works. When Richard said what he did, it cracked the whip for me. And something inside just told me I wasn't going to let it happen, not this time. Richard said I had to get fucking busy, so I got fucking busy."

In particular during the last round, Anissa went into overdrive, punching Lupo furiously, even breaking the other boxer's nose. Still, all told, it was a close fight. But Anissa won the decision. She was now a world champion.

Winning a world title had been her ultimate goal ever since beginning boxing. She used to dream about the elation she would feel once she won a championship. But now that she had one, she couldn't let herself enjoy it. She knew that part of it was that she'd won a vacant title, that she hadn't taken it from a champion. It seemed less significant because of that. But there was more. Anissa says, "I didn't bust my ass for it. I hadn't put 100 percent into the fight from the first round to the last round. I'd just barely pulled it out. So that left me feeling kind of—what?—maybe unfulfilled. I know I almost lost that fight, had to win it in the tenth round. So I wasn't happy. To tell the truth, it was kind of a letdown for me. It was weird."

. . . . .

A year or so after winning the title, Anissa fought again in a Brawl in the Hall for another world title, this one the IFBA junior flyweight title. Her opponent was Wendy Rodriguez from Los Angeles. When Anissa first met Rodriguez at the weigh-in, she thought Wendy looked like a small, innocent child, the least likely person in the world who would hurt you. This helped build Anissa's confidence.

Sweet-faced she may have been, but Rodriguez proved to be a tough fighter who took Anissa a full ten rounds. Still, Anissa was confident she'd won: She believed she landed more scoring blows and that she'd been successful in blocking most of Rodriguez's shots. But the fight was judged a draw. Anissa was dumbfounded. The stunning decision helped Anissa move forward with something she'd been pondering ever since she beat Lupo. Enough was enough. She was leaving boxing.

A lot of things came into play when she decided to retire. Topping the list were the continuous training and nagging injuries; she felt tired and wanted to heal up. But she'd also grown disenchanted with the whole boxing scene. She was ready to get away from the gym. "A lot of people look at the gym from the outside," she once said, "and think we're all one big happy family. Well, if we're a family, we're dysfunctional." She was joking when she said it, but, in fact, there are myriad relationships in any boxing gym, Richard's included. Anissa was at a point at which she wanted to distance herself from a lot of the people who trained at the gym.

She thought it was time to put some space between Richard and herself as well. No relationship in sports quite hits the level of intimacy as that between a boxer and her trainer/manager. In Anissa's case, she'd come to look at Richard as a surrogate father. Richard, for his part, had indeed acted paternally toward her, even to the extent of checking up on her when she was out on dates or partying to make sure she didn't do anything to break training. But now, as a maturing woman approaching thirty, she believed she should start directing her own life a little more.

On top of all that, she'd fallen in love.

CHAPTER EIGHT

*I think maybe some of the people from the gym thought I
should have found a rock star or something instead of just
an Average Joe. But what they don't understand is that an
Average Joe was just what I wanted at the time.*

—ANISSA

· · · · ·

Let's call him Tyler.*
     Anissa met him one day when she stopped by the business he ran with his parents in northwest Austin. She asked if it
would be okay to put up a poster advertising an upcoming Brawl
in the Hall in the window next to the door. Tyler said okay. Then
he and Anissa struck up a brief conversation. He was different
from her—Anglo, older, in the process of ending a bad marriage,
a jeans and T-shirt sort of guy with a decided Texas twang—but
something about him appealed to her, and she decided to stay in
touch. They began dating, and even though they came from different worlds and had different interests, the relationship worked
in its early days.

Tyler was a very good golfer and a tournament pool player, but
he'd never been a boxer or any other sort of athlete who had the
kind of commitment to physical conditioning that Anissa had. For
all the good times they were having together, Anissa could see
from the beginning that boxing was a little intimidating to Tyler
and his family. Early in their relationship, she would invite him to
come to the gym to watch her work out, but he always declined.
He told her eventually he was afraid people would be gawking
at him because he was her boyfriend and she was so well known
around the gym. She understood somewhat. It didn't bother her

that he wasn't a boxer. She never expected him to take up the sport himself. But she was disappointed he never wanted to spend any time at the gym, watching her spar and otherwise do the things she did so well. His doing so would have validated her accomplishments in the ring—and meant a lot to her. When Anissa decided to retire and stopped going to the gym, Tyler and his family felt relieved. Or at least that's how it seemed to Anissa.

She still wanted to live the athlete's lifestyle, rising early, exercising, eating right. But Tyler's business required him to stay up late, and his pastimes involved people who didn't always embrace healthy living. Says Anissa, "I tried to keep in shape after I left boxing. I was pretty nuts about it then. If I gained five pounds, I'd want to do something about it. You know, the fat comes on, well, it's going to come off. Tyler didn't understand that mindset. He'd say stuff like, 'You're just a regular person now. Why can't you act like a regular person?' I know what he was getting at. I'm a lot more laid back about stuff now than I was in my late twenties. But at the time, if I put on a little weight, my thinking was, I don't want to be this kind of person, I don't want to be even a little bit chubby. I still had a lot of boxing notions about diet. I know I went for more than a year after I left the gym without eating any candy. Tyler just couldn't understand that."

As Anissa got to know him better, she came to realize that he could be obsessive about his hobbies, and there were a number of them, everything from ranching to hunting and fishing to golf to playing pool. Once he got involved with Anissa, he began playing in pool tournaments every chance he got. Anissa didn't like the pool hall ambiance—all the cigarette and cigar smoke, the shady characters hustling bets. She eventually stopped going to the tournaments Tyler played in. He went on a short tour at one point and returned home having won a tournament. "Once he did that," Anissa says, "he had a way of putting my name in with it, you know? It was like he was keeping a tally or something. Anissa was a winner and now I'm a winner too—that kind of thing."

Anissa came to believe Tyler felt a need to compete with her every chance he got. If she suggested they go to the Hike and Bike

Trail to ride bikes for a while, Tyler invariably would try to turn it into a race, which was not what Anissa wanted to do at all. On the other hand, she discovered that Tyler couldn't accept any pushing from her when it came to some sort of physical activity. One time they took out a membership at Gold's Gym so they could do some strength training. She says, "When it comes to weight lifting, if I'm trying to get stronger, I'm like doing fifteen reps [repetitions] for one set, then I'm ready to go up in weight. If I get to a weight where I can only do six or eight reps before I give out, I immediately want to pick up some lighter weights and finish the set at fifteen reps. But he wasn't like that. We'd get in so many fights at the gym. He'd be in a set and stop after six or eight reps, and I'd say, 'Pick up some lighter ones and squeeze out another couple of reps.' And he'd get mad at me."

She also discovered that he had not completely gotten over his divorce at the time he started dating her. Sometimes he could act ill-tempered. Anissa learned that kind of behavior usually occurred whenever Tyler was mentally replaying disputes he'd had with his ex-wife when they were still married. At other times, he seemed very insecure and Anissa would try to reassure him that everything was okay. Anissa convinced herself that these problems would heal themselves with the passage of time, but they never did.

Anissa wasn't working when she and Tyler moved in together. She had a lot of time to herself at the house while he was tending to his business. There was a weight set at the house, and sometimes she'd work through some strength-building routines. She'd jump rope, maybe knock out some push-ups and sit-ups. But mostly she was bored. Eventually she took a job at Zen, a popular new restaurant in north Austin that featured inexpensive Japanese food in an informal setting. The job brought in some money, but, more important, it helped her combat boredom.

Says Anissa, "I began to question the relationship. It was driving me nuts. I became like, Is it him or is it me? I think all women kind of go through that stuff when they're in a relationship that's just not going anywhere. I was really questioning myself. You know, I was like, Am I just fucking crazy? Am I doing the right thing being in this relationship? It was weird. And then I went from feeling weird to being depressed. I came to the realization that I didn't really have anything in life at that point except this relationship. I believed I was really trying hard at it. And he wasn't trying at all. I guess because of all that, all my old demons started to come awake again. After a while, I found myself feeling suicidal. It got to the point of where I could be sitting directly across from him and feel as lonely as I've ever felt in my life.

"A regular person. Man, I fucking tried to be a regular person. I tried to do those things a woman is 'supposed' to do. Like I would have his dinner ready for him. I would make his plate for him, keep it warm, all that. But he wouldn't be there at dinnertime. I'd call, and he'd say he'd be there soon, that he was just around the corner. Then he'd get there, get his food, say thanks, then head straight for the garage. For a long time I just kept waiting for things to come back to the way they were when we first got together. I remember the day I stopped trying. I was like, Okay, I don't have to do this anymore. Don't get me wrong: He was a good guy, but we weren't good together."

· · · · ·

It had been nearly two years since she left Richard Lord's Boxing Gym for the last time. She hadn't talked to Richard at all during that time. On occasion she'd hear from Lori, but for the most part the boxing gym had been shut out of her life. She made little effort to stay in touch with most of the other boxers, and she did not communicate with Richard. She knew he must have been perplexed by that, but she knew something Richard didn't know: If she'd as much as exchanged a short conversation with Richard, she'd want to resume her boxing career again. So she'd kept her distance from him, both because she believed she needed to stay away from boxing for a while and because she knew a return to boxing would doom her relationship with Tyler.

But with that relationship in ruins, she picked up the phone and dialed the gym. When Richard answered, she told him she wanted to start boxing again. He told her to come on back to the gym.

If Tyler had any illusions about the health of the relationship, they were smashed as soon as Anissa began training again. When Anissa told him she was leaving, Tyler said, "I'm not going to come chasing you."

"That's okay," Anissa replied.

Then, after a pause, Tyler said, "Well, tell Richard he won."

Anissa shook her head. So that's how he looked at it. She didn't know there had been some sort of competition going on over her. She was sure Richard didn't know it either. Tyler's saying it pretty much summed up everything wrong with the relationship. She left knowing she was doing the right thing.

She'd had enough of being a regular person.

. . . . .

Anissa's mom had retired from IBM and was living in a small apartment. Anissa moved in with her and organized her days around working at Zen and training to return to the ring. The suicidal thoughts that had troubled her began to recede as she threw herself back into fitness routines. She knew she would have to work hard after a two-year layoff to get back to where she'd been when she retired. But now she believed she was more directed than she'd ever been in the first part of her career.

She was especially mindful of the fights she should have won but lost because her head wasn't in the right place. She now understood that if she'd just adjusted her attitude, she could have won those fights. Losing because of homecookin' in another fighter's favor was one thing. Losing to an opponent who was a more experienced boxer with better skills was acceptable too. But giving up a decision because of her mindset, that was something she never wanted to tolerate again. She dreamed of fighting ten rounds in which she would be at the top of her game for each second she was in the ring, never allowing "fuck it, who cares?" thinking to spoil any of it. She wasn't sure she'd be able to pull it off, but she was going to give it her damnedest.

. . . . .

On May 17, 2002, Anissa fought before an audience for the first time since she'd retired, taking part in a boxing exhibition at the Austin Convention Center against Isabel Manyseng and a young up-and-comer named Maribel Zurita. She received an enthusiastic welcome from the hometown audience, even if it was clear she was not the boxer she'd been back in 1999 when she'd won her world title.

Of particular interest were her rounds with Zurita. Six months earlier, Zurita had faced Jay Vega, whom Richard trained and managed, in a four-round bout at the Frank Erwin Center in Austin. It was Zurita's second pro fight, and Vega won a relatively easy unanimous decision. But even in losing, Zurita delighted the crowd with her ring energy and made a name for herself among Austin fight fans. Since then, she'd fought three times, scoring a draw in the first before winning two in a row. When she met Anissa in their exhibition rounds, she fought much better than she had against Vega.

As for Anissa, she felt strange boxing again after so long an absence. She was nervous, more nervous than she could remember being in any other fight, even though this one was just an exhibition. Nothing seemed to be coming back to her very easily. She remembered how she used to feel a certain level of comfort whenever she climbed into the ring during the first part of her career. That was all gone now, replaced by awkwardness. Looking back on that night, she says, "I hadn't really even been training in the gym that much before I fought those exhibition rounds. I hadn't had that much sparring. You know, when you spar, you do all these things over and over to the point to where you can do them without thinking. But I hadn't had enough sparring to be at that place yet. And I was still working on bringing my body back in shape. My performance that night—it wasn't pretty."

Anissa had six months between the exhibition and her first "real" fight to try to get things prettier. She thought she'd improved a lot when she and Richard traveled to Mercedes, Texas, in the Rio Grande Valley. Anissa remembers it as a "long-assed drive" that had a surprise waiting at the end of it, where her opponent, Andrea Benitez from Mexico, was an experienced fighter who retired and was making a comeback. The surprise? Benitez was a left-handed fighter, something that neither Richard nor Anissa knew until they saw her signing paperwork at the weigh-in.

"Wait a minute, she's a southpaw," Richard said to Anissa.

Anissa responded with "Oh, shit."

In the first part of her career, she had, of course, fought Eva Jones-Young, who was left-handed, so it wasn't a new experience for Anissa. But right-handed boxers prepare for southpaws by sparring round after round with left-handed sparring partners in the weeks before they fight. Anissa had not done this to get ready for Benitez. Moreover, Benitez was a good boxer, or, as Anissa recalls, "She had some spunk to her."

Nevertheless, Anissa won the fight at the Tejano Ballroom with a four-round majority decision. It wasn't a strong performance by Anissa, but it was the first fight of record since her comeback, and it was a win and a win away from home. In fact, Anissa preferred fighting away from home for her official return to the ring; she didn't want to feel pressured to live up to the expectations of a hometown crowd. "It was perfect, in a way," she says. "I got the ring rust off me and I was able to do what I needed to do." And it was against an opponent who was no pushover.

Just a month later Anissa took a voyage that dwarfed the long, boring drive to the Valley and back. She and Richard flew eight thousand miles to the tiny Pacific island of Guam, a speck on the globe known to most Americans for the military bases located there and for the preponderance of poisonous brown tree snakes (accidentally introduced by the U.S. Navy) now found on the once snake-free island.

Her opponent was Yvonne Tara Caples, a native of Pune, India, who'd taken up boxing while enrolled at the University of California, Berkeley. Caples had grown up in a household in which women were encouraged to pursue sports. Her mother competed in pentathlons as a young woman and later played racquetball and tennis, with her opponents frequently male. "She didn't just want to be the best *female* athlete out on the court," Caples said of her mother. "She wanted to be the best athlete, period." After graduating from Berkeley, Caples became a high school English teacher and eventually coached boxing at her alma mater. She fought seventeen amateur fights before turning pro, winning thirteen of them, including the 106-pound title fight in the first-ever national Golden Gloves tournament for women.

Caples's pro career, however, got off to a shaky start. After five fights, her record stood at 2-3, including a ten-round unanimous decision loss to Lori Lord at Austin's Ben Hur Shrine Temple in August 2000. After that, she had five straight fights without a defeat (four wins and one draw). Then she traveled to Germany to fight Regina Halmich in Berlin for the WIBF junior flyweight world title. Halmich won a highly controversial decision to move her pro record to an impressive 40-1-0. Caples and her fans believed she had clearly won the fight; even Halmich's hometown audience in Berlin thought Caples had been robbed. The ring announcer received boos and whistles as he read the decision. Caples's record stood at 6-4-1 when she signed up to fight Anissa in a ten-round match.

"It was a damn long flight to a very small place," Anissa says of the trip, "a place where absolutely nothing was happening. I'm not sure why they wanted to promote a female boxing match on Guam, but they did, and we went." She and Richard arrived in Agana the day before the fight and drove out to the field house at Guam University to inspect the ring, both of them extremely disoriented by jet lag. On top of that, the promoters didn't quite seem to understand how to put on a fight card. The one good piece of news was that her match with Caples was not scheduled until very late the next night. It would give her some time to pull herself together.

Caples was a left-hander like Benitez, so Anissa was glad she'd had the fight against her as preparation for Caples. As the fight began, Anissa discovered that Caples was going to move around a lot. That opened the door for Anissa to play the aggressor, which was just fine with her. She had no trouble keeping up with Caples, popping her every chance she got. At the halfway point, Anissa felt herself getting back into her old groove for the first time since she'd emerged from retirement. Everything was coming together for her just right.

It was in the fifth round that Anissa connected with a hard right hook. Immediately after the hook landed, her head collided with Caples's, opening a bad cut on Caples's forehead. Once Anissa saw the blood, she went to work on the cut, splitting it wider and wider. Then, suddenly, the referee separated the two women. Anissa had her head so far into the fight she wasn't sure exactly what was happening. Then she realized she'd just been awarded a TKO victory over Caples. Anissa was shocked. She didn't think Caples's injury was bad enough to stop the fight. And Caples sure as hell wasn't happy about it. But the ref made the decision and Anissa boarded the plane for the long flight back to Austin with a victory.

. . . . .

Each winter, Richard Lord produces a sort of modern-day equivalent of a smoker for Austin-area Realtors. It's a high-dollar affair that occurs in swanky surroundings, and in February 2003, it occurred at the Renaissance Hotel in northwest Austin. Anissa fought Maribel Zurita in that year's edition of the smoker. Zurita, still finding her bearings as a fighter, brought a record of 4-3-1 into the match. Like Anissa, she'd last fought in November, when she lost a unanimous decision to Patricia Martinez in Miami. But even in losing, Zurita had won the fans' respect. While Zurita could not punch as accurately as Martinez, she showed a great deal of pluck in the fight and boxed gamely through the final round. The audience gave both fighters rousing applause after the decision was announced.

As an improving young boxer with plenty of spirit and drive,

Zurita presented a challenge to Anissa, who wasn't in the best of shape to fight the younger boxer: "The biggest thing I remember is that I didn't really train for it. I'd just come off the holidays, you know? I'd gained some weight and I really hadn't put my mind back into boxing yet. Another thing I remember was how cold it was. I mean, the weather had turned cold and the gym was freezing, so it was hard for me to really get myself pumped up for working out. And I remember I wasn't running the way I should have been, so I was a little short on stamina."

Zurita, on the other hand, arrived in Austin in prime condition and ready to fight. In the end, Anissa defeated her in a split decision—"I won by the hair of my chinny-chin-chin"—and she learned a lesson. She needed to pay more attention to her conditioning if she was going to continue to be successful in the ring.

That August, she was scheduled to fight Zurita again. She knew she had to be better prepared for this fight. Zurita's manager, Tony Ayala, had openly expressed his contempt for the decision in the first Zamarron-Zurita fight. Anissa believed she needed a strong win at the Austin Convention Center that summer to convince any doubters. But as it turned out, Zurita was unable to fight, and Stephanie Dobbs appeared as her substitute on the card.

Dobbs was nearly a decade younger than Anissa. She came from the Oklahoma City suburb of Moore and had been boxing since she was twenty-one. She entered the pro ranks with no amateur experience. Consequently, she lost a number of her early fights as she learned the art of boxing, but that didn't seem to deter her. She seemed willing and ready to fight whoever was available, novices and world champions alike, in venues ranging from barbecue joints to farmers markets to large auditoriums. Her pace never appeared to slow down. When she fought Anissa, Dobbs had a record of 8-14-2.

Anissa went into the fight believing she'd upped her skills. She'd been working out under the tutelage of Flaco Castrejon, an outstanding young trainer who'd recently arrived at Richard's gym by way of Jesus Chavez. During his exile from American boxing, Chavez had trained under Castrejon in Mexico City. Once

Chavez's deportation was lifted, he persuaded Castrejon to join him in Austin. Castrejon began working the corner with Richard during Chavez's fights. Eventually Castrejon trained a number of Austin-area boxers and even opened his own gym. But when he worked with Anissa he was still largely unknown and he had a lot of time to devote to her. Their training sessions were a little awkward, for Flaco spoke hardly any English, while Anissa knew only a few words of Spanish. But through gestures, they got a lot of work done, even if Anissa didn't quite understand at the time what the payoff might be. Flaco took her back to the basics, beginning with the first punch a boxer learns to throw: the jab. Flaco improvised a training regimen that involved Anissa standing in front of a block of wood and throwing jab after jab at it until her left arm was throbbing.

Says Anissa: "It was a great deal for me. I don't know exactly what the arrangement was with Jesus at the time, but Flaco didn't ask for any money to train me. It was all taken care of, thanks to Jesus. There was no way I could have afforded to hire a trainer as good as Flaco. I realized it was a great opportunity for me, so I tried to soak up everything Flaco had to say. Flaco had me do all these drills, over and over and over. When you're doing them, you're thinking, Why am I doing this crap so many times? What's the point? Then, one day, you're doing this stuff, and it all clicks. It suddenly makes sense. I didn't really understand that what a lot of people call instinct is really just stuff that you practice over and over until you do it without thinking.

"In the early part of my career, when I'd get into a fight, I'd just be throwing and reacting and my nerves would be out of control. I just did what happened, if that makes sense. But after working with Flaco, I started to get things under control. I knew what was happening. When I fought Stephanie, I just started doing things Flaco taught me, without giving it any thought. Like, she'd throw down on me and I'd just automatically move laterally so she wouldn't hit me. And then I'd find myself at an angle where I could attack her."

Her improved tactical skills worked to Anissa's advantage, as she defeated Dobbs by unanimous decision. She continued to focus on technique over the next six months, and when she fought Maribel Zurita for their second fight of record, she won, this time by unanimous decision. Tony Ayala made his claim that Zurita had beat Anissa "from pillar to post," and Anissa admits it was a close fight—close, but, unlike their first fight, one she clearly won. "Ayala and them threw a fit about it," Anissa says, "but there were no ifs, ands, or buts about it. I won. It was close, but it wasn't really that tough a fight for me. I don't know where Ayala was coming from."

Anissa had little time to bask in the victory. In fact, that win faded quickly as Anissa began a string of bouts facing fighters she would consider among the very best she'd ever fought. Anissa lost every one of them.

· · · · ·

A month after defeating Zurita for a second time, Anissa traveled U.S. 290 from Austin to Houston, where she fought Johanna "La Bailarina" Pena Alvarez of the Dominican Republic. The left-handed Pena was coming off a ten-round loss to Regina Halmich, only the second defeat of her career against fourteen victories. Pena was just twenty-one years old, but already had four years of professional boxing under her belt. She dominated Anissa throughout the fight, winning a clear-cut unanimous decision, and in so doing she took from Anissa the Texas flyweight title that Anissa had claimed by beating Zurita a month earlier.

In May 2004, Anissa stepped into the ring against Wendy Rodriguez, whom she'd first fought four years earlier. This time the fight took place in Grand Casino Coushatta in Kinder, Louisiana, and the winner would be declared the North American Boxing Association—Female junior flyweight world champion. Anissa began well, winning the first round, and at times she had Rodriguez against the ropes later in the fight. But Rodriguez proved to be the better boxer that night and won a unanimous ten-round decision. But there was more to the story.

After the weigh-in prior to the fight, Richard and Anissa had gone to a restaurant. Anissa felt particularly hungry and opted to eat from the buffet, although Richard typically advised her to avoid buffets—you never know how long the food's been sitting out. Richard's fears proved valid in this instance. Anissa came down with food poisoning and she was vomiting and suffered intense diarrhea the next day while running a high fever. Somehow, though, she got herself ready to fight. She hardly weighed a hundred pounds when she climbed into the ring, dehydrated and exhausted before the bell even rang. Though she lost, Richard thought Anissa's going through with that match was one of the bravest performances he'd ever experienced in his years as a trainer and manager.

Anissa did not fight again until January 2005. This time her opponent was Melinda Cooper of Las Vegas, who'd begun boxing as an amateur at age eleven. When she was fifteen, she won a USA Boxing national championship and the next year she won a national Golden Gloves title. In all, she had thirty-nine amateur fights, winning thirty-seven of them. Her victorious ways continued unabated after she turned pro at age seventeen. Over two years, she racked up thirteen straight victories, including seven knockouts. One of her best wins was a unanimous six-round decision over Johanna Pena Alvarez.

Cooper had not yet turned twenty years old when she fought Anissa in Rancho Mirage, California. In many ways, Cooper epitomized Anissa's hopes for the future of women's boxing. Cooper was a talented athlete who began fighting very young, just as the best male boxers start learning very young. She'd had a rich amateur career to prepare for boxing professionally. She was not a brawler. Under the tutelage of skilled trainers, she'd mastered the fundamentals of the sweet science. She was the complete package. Anissa considers her the best boxer she ever fought.

Anissa made it through eight full rounds, fighting gamely while absorbing some very heavy punches. At times, Anissa used her experience to get the upper hand on Cooper, but Cooper found ways to regain the advantage. Well-schooled boxer that she was,

Cooper began to score heavily with fast combinations in the later rounds. Thirty-nine seconds into the ninth round, the referee had seen enough. He stopped the fight and gave the victory to Cooper on a technical knockout. It was an unfortunate first for Anissa. Never before had she been TKO'd.

In March, Anissa went to Louisiana for a third clash with Wendy Rodriguez, this time at the Paragon Casino Resort in Marksville. Rodriguez clearly outfought Anissa, smacking her with hard right counterpunches. Through some of the rounds, Anissa seemed clueless about how to respond to Rodriguez. In the fifth, Rodriguez slugged her repeatedly with straight rights, one of those a hard shot to the nose followed by a brutal right-left combination while Anissa was pinned against the ropes. It appeared for a moment that Anissa might collapse, but somehow she dug down deep inside herself and survived the round. She finished the fight, although the decision was never in question. The judges' scorecards show it was the most lopsided unanimous loss of her career. Anissa looked battered, red-faced, and totally exhausted at the end of the fight. Rodriguez, on the other hand, showed no bruises or abrasions and seemed to have enough energy left to fight another ten rounds.

Anissa's record fell to 16-14-2. Friends concerned about her physical well-being began to whisper behind her back that she should retire before she suffered serious damage in the ring. If not for her health, their reasoning went, she should quit before she frittered away her winning career record, since she now had only two more victories than defeats. But what virtually no one knew at the time was that Anissa had never been completely satisfied with any of her boxing performances so far. She knew she could do better.

· · · · ·

The best-known female boxer from Austin during Anissa's career did not train at Richard Lord's Boxing Gym. She was Ann Wolfe, a fearsome super middleweight/light heavyweight who would claim world championships from three sanctioning organizations. She gained fame outside the ring not for posing in girly magazines but for her willingness to fight any comers, even if they were male. She achieved a great deal of notoriety outside boxing when she fought *Esquire* magazine writer Scott Raab in a three-round exhibition. Raab outweighed her by some seventy-five pounds, yet Wolfe gave him a standing eight-count in the first round and wobbled him at other times in the fight with her power shots. She also received a lot of press as promoters tried to make a match between her and Laila Ali, daughter of Muhammad Ali; Laila Ali, a talented boxer, seemed reluctant to get in the ring with Wolfe, and the match never was made.

Behind the newspaper headlines and magazine articles about Wolfe is one of the most heartrending stories to be found in American sports. Both her father and her brother were victims of murder. When Wolfe was in the sixth grade, she dropped out of school to care for her cancer-stricken mother, who succumbed to the disease when Wolfe was eighteen. For a year, Wolfe was homeless, living on the streets with her two daughters. As a street person, she learned to fistfight to protect both herself and her daughters. She also developed expertise as a thief to provide for her family, and trouble with the law ensued. Eventually she found her way to the East Austin gym of Donald "Pops" Billingsly, a kindhearted, churchgoing boxing trainer who occasionally brings his fighters to Lord's gym for sparring. Under Pops's tutelage, she learned boxing in a ten-foot homemade ring.

As one might expect, Wolfe and Anissa are simpatico with each other. "She's been real smart," Anissa says of Wolfe, "and she always gave me good advice. It was coming to a point where I really wasn't seeing any results as far as advancing in my career, not to mention my life. I was getting kind of bitter because I just didn't see any reward. I just felt lost. One day Ann was at the gym and I was feeling really down and she told me, 'Don't leave this sport with nothing.'"

Don't leave this sport with nothing. Those words resonated with Anissa as she faced the close of her career. Then she had the chance to fight Maribel Zurita for a world championship. Before she left the sport, Anissa wanted one fight where she was able to put everything together: Get her conditioning in the right place, hone her boxing skills to their sharpest level, step into the ring mentally tough.

Her third fight with Maribel provided the opportunity for her to do that. And she pulled it off.

EPILOGUE

NEVER KNOCKED OUT

In 2005, the same year that Anissa defeated Maribel Zurita to claim her second world championship, the World Boxing Council began to rank female boxers. The WBC was created in 1963 as an international organization to sanction professional boxing matches and recognize champions; prior to the WBC, male boxing champions were crowned as such by noninternational groups like the New York State Athletic Commission or the British Boxing Board of Control or by magazines such as *The Ring*. Since its inception, the WBC arguably has been the most respected sanctioning organization in professional boxing, although it receives competition from the World Boxing Association (WBA) and the International Boxing Federation (IBF), and, like the other two organizations, has been criticized for corruption.

Anissa was excited by the WBC's recognition of women's boxing. To her, it meant women's boxing truly had become big-time, something more than just a sideshow. And she believed she had done her part to elevate the sport to this new level of legitimacy and took satisfaction in that. But Anissa also knew her career could not last much longer, given her age. She decided she had one last goal to achieve before exiting the boxing ring for the last time: She wanted to fight for a WBC title.

Her chances looked good. The May 2005 initial WBC rankings listed her as seventh in the world in her weight category. After she defeated Zurita, she rose to fifth. As a top-five contender, she thought a title shot was within reach. So she began conditioning herself to fight again.

But Anissa's training ended before it really began. One Saturday morning at Richard's gym, she entered the ring to spar, never thinking disaster might occur. She didn't attempt anything unusual or particularly strenuous that day, but without warning, as she glided around the ring, a searing pain shot through her knee. She fell to the canvas, screaming, and, by her own admission, shouting every obscenity under the sun. The injury was bad: She'd torn an anterior cruciate ligament (ACL) again and she needed surgery.

She didn't realize it at the time, but her boxing career ended that morning.

Anissa also didn't realize that the demons she had been keeping at bay for so long would reawaken with a fury with that injury.

· · · · ·

When Anissa and I began collaborating on this book, I thought it would be a fairly straightforward success story: Troubled young woman finds redemption through boxing and has a message of inspiration for all people but especially for young Hispanic women who feel trapped by the circumstances of their lives. I should have known better. Real-life stories are seldom, if ever, that simple.

I had known Anissa for several years before we started on the book. I was (and am) a regular at Richard Lord's Boxing Gym, a middle-age man attempting to learn a sport that's far from easy to master. (This is especially true when you're a person such as myself possessing scarcely any natural athletic ability.) Of course, I never had any illusions about actually boxing competitively, but I was a lifelong fan of boxing and I loved training at the gym, banging away at the bags, performing mitt drills, occasionally sparring, and enduring murderous sessions involving Richard and a medicine ball.

I'd see Anissa, or at least her image, as soon as I pulled into the gym parking lot. For years a statue of her was perched atop the gym. Before going inside, I'd always pause a moment to study that statue. It was somewhat more impressionistic than realistic, but anyone who knew her could tell it represented Anissa. The figure was compact, tight, tough, done up in boxing gear—a hard-hitting chick ready for battle. And there was a great deal of determined strength in the face. Yet at the same time her expression was one of friendliness, and the artist captured Anissa's smile, which can be as infectious as any smile I've ever seen. I always thought that statue summed up not only Anissa but the ambiance of the gym as well.

I was always glad to see the real-life Anissa inside the gym. I learned as I got to know her that she could be many things at once. When I watched her sparring or, more so, when I watched her in an actual fight, she impressed me as a fierce, take-no-prisoners competitor. I also learned that outside the ring she can be a loyal, supportive friend, a good person to share some laughs with over a beer or two. And I learned you could witness both those aspects of her personality on the same day. Some days at the gym she seemed to be really focused on her training and didn't want to get sidetracked by anything else. Other days, she was up for the sort of tomfoolery some of us engage in there regularly. At times she seemed to be carrying a heavy burden of some sort. At others, she seemed carefree as the wind. But wherever her head was, I always liked talking to her. And I always liked watching her in the ring. Comparing male and female boxers is risky business, but I can say I never saw another Austin fighter, not even Jesus Chavez, who moved with more athletic grace than Anissa.

As I came to know more about women's boxing, my appreciation of Anissa grew even larger. She was part of a generation of female fighters who created a kind of golden age for the sport back in the 1990s. Anissa told me that one of the things she wanted to accomplish during her career (which ended up covering a dozen years) was to help create a future for female athletes who want to pursue boxing as a legitimate sport. She and the other serious boxers of her generation have accomplished this goal. Women's boxing is here to stay. For her role in that, she has every right to be proud.

I felt honored when Anissa asked me to work with her on telling her story. It turned out to be a challenging undertaking for me, because Anissa is someone I care about. It was difficult for me to hear her tell of what she endured during her worst times. And it was even more difficult for me to witness firsthand what she suffered through after she tore her ACL in the gym that Saturday morning.

About the time of that surgery, Anissa's statue disappeared from the roof of the gym. It stood for a while in the back room, then was taken away to be repaired. It seems fitting, from a symbolic point of view, for it to be gone, for Anissa herself was absent from the gym for a long time.

. . . . .

Anissa's ACL surgery was performed by Ted Spears, a noted orthopedic surgeon in Austin with a reputation for treating athletes with an eye toward keeping them active in their sports. The surgery went well, and Anissa hit it off with Spears, a fifth-generation Texan originally from Abilene, to the extent that he offered her a job as a part-time medical receptionist at his clinic, Sports Performance International. Their friendship developed beyond the workplace in the ensuing months.

Spears and his wife, Rita, were dedicated distance runners. Spears had started jogging three decades earlier during his first year of study at the University of Texas Medical Branch in Galveston in an effort to kick cigarette smoking. He met Rita in the 1980s while practicing orthopedics in Houston. They married in 1986 and honeymooned by taking part in that year's San Francisco Marathon. While Ted continued to run marathons and to conduct running clinics, it was Rita who distinguished herself in the sport by qualifying for the Boston Marathon three times. The way Ted and Rita had incorporated running into their family and professional lives appealed to Anissa. For their part, the Spearses took a liking to Anissa and occasionally invited her to take part in family get-togethers.

As an older, experienced, successful man, Spears functioned as a source of advice and guidance for Anissa for matters beyond work and physical fitness. Ted and Rita were devout Christians, as were some other employees at Sports Performance International. As she healed from the ACL surgery, Anissa found herself undergoing a spiritual awakening. She knew little about the Bible or what various churches might have to offer, and she wanted to explore options for filling the spiritual void she now sensed in herself. Churches with evangelical leanings appealed to her; the Catholic Church that she'd known during her childhood was not the right answer for her as an adult. So with the Spearses or with friends from work or with Lori Lord, she attended different churches, listened to their messages, and contemplated which path would be the best for her. She was particularly moved by a visit she and Ted made to the Church Under the Bridge, a nondenominational praise service for homeless people held on Sunday mornings under an Interstate 35 overpass in downtown Austin. Anissa decided the Church Under the Bridge was a project into which she wanted to invest herself.

But this goal, like others she had at the time, wound up on a sidetrack as Anissa fought her way through grim times.

. . . . .

In retrospect, Anissa believes she tried to come back too quickly from her knee surgery. She began running again but wound up with a reinjured knee, requiring more surgery. This time the surgery included repairs to a damaged ankle. Meanwhile, she also had discovered that the years of repetitive stress through boxing had damaged her left shoulder. All told, over a period of about eighteen months, Anissa endured two knee surgeries, one ankle surgery, and two shoulder surgeries. Her tendency to suffer muscle and ligament tears led Lori Lord to speculate that spending so much time immobilized on a bed during her adolescent years had adversely affected Anissa's physical development, leaving her more prone to injury than most people.

Maybe so. Whatever the underlying causes of the injuries, the surgeries to repair them forced Anissa to give up her active lifestyle for a long period of time. What's more, it became apparent that she could never box again; her body simply could no longer stand the wear and tear. This had a devastating effect on her emotional well-being. Before she fully comprehended what was happening, she found herself mired in perhaps the worst psychological morass she'd encountered since those darks days of heavy substance abuse after exiting Brookhaven two decades earlier.

Not all the news was bad. A full-time position opened at the clinic and Anissa filled it, giving her access to much-needed health insurance. But there also were tough times at work. With her boxing background, Anissa had been inclined to blurt out whatever crossed her mind, regardless of where she was. This didn't play well in an office environment. Moreover, her problems with attention deficit/hyperactivity disorder flared up again. One week the office manager put the entire staff on probation, but Anissa told me the work problems that prompted the probation were almost entirely hers, not her coworkers'.

Sensing she had to take steps to get her life under control, Anissa sought and received a referral to a psychiatrist, who prescribed two drugs: a mood stabilizer and another to address the ADHD symptoms. As is usually the case with psychotropic drugs, it took a while to get the doses right. Once that was achieved, however, Anissa began to feel better. And just in time. Before going to the psychiatrist for treatment, she'd slipped so far downward that she had been fantasizing about suicide.

"You know, it's like I'll be driving in my car on the highway," she told me one day, "and I'll be passing a truck. I find myself edging closer and closer to the truck, and I'm thinking, Yeah, I could do this. Or I'll be at my apartment or someplace else, and I'll look around and see just how I could go about hanging myself."

I felt myself shudder as she described further details of her suicidal fantasies.

But with the drugs working effectively, it seemed as if a crisis had been averted. Anissa was taking long walks and even returned to the boxing gym to work out a little. Even though she was limited as to what she could do, I was glad to see her back at Richard

Lord's place. The gym didn't seem quite complete unless Anissa was around.

Then I didn't see or hear from her for a few days, and I asked Richard about her. "You haven't heard?" he said. "She's in the hospital. Emergency surgery."

I got the full story from Anissa over the telephone later. For some time, she had been suffering from abdominal pain. She'd seen a male doctor about it, who ordered tests followed by plans for surgery down the line a few days. But before that date even got close, Anissa was in such pain that she could not stand up straight; beyond that, she was unable to urinate. She went to an emergency clinic, where she saw a female gynecologist who was chagrinned by the male doctor's seemingly lackadaisical approach to addressing the issue. She ordered Anissa into surgery immediately, even though Anissa had not been fasting: "I was throwing up all over the place," she told me.

Two ovarian cysts were removed during the surgery, one the size of a grapefruit. The cysts had been constricting her ovaries, and had the surgery not taken place when it did, there was a chance she might have lost one if not both of them. Now, as she spoke to me over the telephone shortly after leaving the hospital, she was concerned about the scar. I tried to reassure her. It was too early to know what kind of scar would remain for the long term. After a year, it would be much less noticeable than it was now, I speculated. She then wondered aloud if the cysts might have altered her body chemistry, knocking her hormones out of whack, and if that were the case, could it have affected her emotions, maybe contributing to the craziness she'd been enduring? Wouldn't surprise me, I replied.

She told me she was feeling a little antsy. Because of the surgery, she'd gone off her meds for the mood disorder and ADHD. But she planned to go back on them. She hoped, now that the cysts had been taken care of and the psychiatrist had come up with an effective drug cocktail for her mental issues, things would settle down for her.

She rang off. I walked to a window, peered out at my front yard, and pondered all she'd gone through in her extraordinary life. The load she had carried for so many years was staggering. I felt sure I could not have borne it. For one thing, I don't possess the physical or mental fortitude to have fought in thirty-three professional boxing matches. But Anissa handled it, managing even to come back from a string of losses to upset a world champion and take her title. But boxing, difficult as it is, was not the most taxing obstacle she'd confronted. Far from it. She was able to plow through impediments that would have defeated me. And most other people as well.

. . . . .

My hope that she would enjoy a period of calm was soon dashed.

One day I came home and checked my voice mail. The caller ID showed that someone from Austin's Seton Medical Center had dialed my number during the day, but there was no message. My stepdaughter, Kim, is an RN at one of the Seton hospitals, so I figured she might have been the caller, although she usually calls on her cell phone, even when she's at work. The next day, there was another call from Seton, and again there was no voice mail from the caller. Perplexed, I decided this was not a call from Kim. Maybe Seton was involved in some sort of telemarketing, I decided. Later that day, the phone rang and caller ID showed it was yet another Seton call. Although I felt certain it would be somebody trying to sell me something, I went ahead and answered.

"Kip," said a distinctive and familiar voice. "It's 'Nissa."

"Anissa?"

"Yeah, I guess you know where I am."

"Well, the caller ID says Seton."

"Seton? Well, I'm in Shoal Creek."

Of course, Shoal Creek. I'd forgotten Shoal Creek was part of the Seton system of hospitals. As the realization of what a call from Anissa at Shoal Creek meant, I felt my spirits sink.

"Oh no," I said.

"Yeah, I've been here a couple of days."

All I could come up with to say was "Oh no" again.

"But I'm doing okay."

"Yeah?"

"Yeah . . ."

Things had spun completely out of control in her life as she was recovering from the ovarian cyst surgery. She had no focus at work and was acting erratically, creating turmoil among her coworkers. She had become suicidal once more. And, more than fifteen years after the last time she'd done it, she began cutting herself again.

A couple of weeks earlier, she had accompanied Richard and Lori Lord to a friend's ranch, where they'd spent an afternoon zipping across the countryside in all-terrain vehicles. Anissa picked up a laceration on her wrist from a low-hanging branch as the ATV she was riding roared past a mesquite. When she got back to Austin, she examined the wound on her wrist and long-dormant urges began to overtake her.

Rationalizing that no one would notice if she only cut herself a little, making the already existing injury a little bigger, she did just that. She shivered with a twisted kind of joy as she made herself bleed, feeling in charge at last after battling so many things she could not control, getting a rush from the release of endorphins that accompanied the pain. "It was a real fucking high," she told me later.

I remembered that during a crazy time just prior to the cyst surgery, she had nervously chewed her nails down to nubs. Her fingers looked terrible, and I'm sure she must have bled when she was biting her nails. I decided that must have been a prelude to her decision to start cutting again.

I asked her how much longer she would be in Shoal Creek. She said probably just a few more days before she began an out-patient program. Could I come see her? Sure, she said. She gave me a numeric code that gave me authorization to visit or call her. At noon the next day, a Sunday, I went to Shoal Creek.

I drove to the nondescript building in north-central Austin, just a few blocks from Seton's home campus. As I pulled off Thirty-fifth Street, I passed the supermarket and the Taco Bell (now closed) to which Anissa would receive passes when she was a teenage patient at Shoal Creek more than twenty years earlier. I parked in the lot, and, following Anissa's instructions, emptied my pockets of everything except my car keys. The main entrance was closed for remodeling, so I followed the temporary signs that led to a side door. I joined a line of people waiting to be processed by the security officer so they could get inside to visit patients.

I was nervous as I stood on the sidewalk. In high school, I'd taken part in my psychology class's field trip to Central State Hospital, the large mental hospital in Norman, Oklahoma. As a seventeen-year-old, I was exposed to a *Snake Pit* nightmare of acute patients wildly gesticulating and cursing themselves while silent chronics stood in puddles of their own urine and staff members moved about seemingly unconcerned about the plight of their charges. Or at least that's how it appeared to my inexperienced eyes. Thirty years later, those images remained burned in my memory. I'd resolved way back then never to darken the doorway of a mental hospital again. For three decades I'd kept that resolution. Now I was getting ready to break it.

The line began to move. When I reached the security guard, he asked me whom I'd come to visit. I told him. He then asked for the code. The code synched with her name on his list, so he had me sign in. He told me she was on the third floor and directed me to the elevator. As I walked down the hall, I detected an odor much like what you find in nursing homes, and I flashed on those chronics standing in their own piss back in the mid-1970s at Central State Hospital. I feared I would encounter something like that again.

But I didn't.

The staff opened the locked door to admit me to the ward on the third floor, where I signed in again. There was a good deal of activity with friends and family of patients, as well as the patients themselves rushing about for visiting hour. With one or two exceptions, the patients I saw wore street clothes. The ward itself was shy on homey touches; think "institutional décor," with all its inherit drabness, and you pretty well have Shoal Creek. But it seemed clean enough and certainly none of the patients appeared to be neglected.

Anissa's friend from work, Maryjane,* had beat me there. I asked her how Anissa was doing. "Not too well right now," Maryjane said.

Then I spotted Anissa. She was wearing a short-sleeved shirt, jeans, and Converse Chuck Taylor All-Stars, minus the laces. She was marching up and down the hall, with every aspect of her body language suggesting she was one pissed-off woman. Anissa saw me, and she walked over to me and said, "Hey, Kip." We hugged and for a moment she seemed glad to see me. Then whatever had made her angry overtook her again and she stomped away.

When she returned she invited Maryjane and me into the room she shared with another female patient. I sat on her bed and learned why she was fuming: a dispute with a security guard over the delivery of some food from Taco Bell. Anissa was counting on that for lunch because, unable to stomach the institutional food at Shoal Creek, she hadn't been eating. Anissa was livid with the guard.

"I'm going to get that motherfucker," Anissa seethed. "I know how to get down there. I can take him down."

"Anissa," I said, "you don't want to be saying shit like that. They'll put you back in PICU." I knew that Anissa had spent her first days of this Shoal Creek visit in the psychiatric ICU after she'd cut herself on the ward, using a plastic meal service knife.

"I'm going to get him," she said, simmering. "I'm going to get him."

Maryjane excused herself.

"So tell me what happened," I said.

She told me that she now realized that a demon was back in her emotional life and she'd had bouts of dealing with it for some time. "It seemed like every time I tried to walk back into the gym, one of my limbs was falling off. I was about ready to step it up in terms of training, and something else would happen. I think that all of that came to a head. I think that I always battled this demon from time to time, even during my boxing career. I thought I kept it pretty well hidden, under control, but I guess not. To tell the truth, I have always been very moody and very difficult to be around at times. So when I was finally getting the true effects of the Trileptal [a drug primarily used to treat epilepsy, but also sometimes prescribed for people suffering from bipolarism and mood disorders], I was feeling really good, and for the first time I was actually stable. I mean, I didn't feel like everything was great in the world, but I felt okay.

"But then I had the cyst surgery and went off my meds and everything got really crazy. And I started cutting myself. I told Maryjane about it because I did want help and I needed to find a therapist. We checked around and every therapist said they weren't accepting new patients. So the thing about it at Shoal Creek—I thought they couldn't just let me go, they would have to help me find a therapist. They can't just throw you out on your ass.

"It was on a Thursday and Maryjane took me to Shoal Creek. We stopped at my apartment, I picked up some clothes, and she was going to take care of my dog. I wasn't really happy about it. It was weighing heavy on my mind about going to Shoal Creek. It is really different now from the last time I was here. So we get here and they take me up to the fifth floor, which is the admissions floor. Now, it takes something like three to five hours to get admitted because they have to observe you and evaluate you. After a while, I said, 'Oh fuck it, I ain't staying here!' I just grabbed my stuff and I jumped in the elevator and there was nobody to stop me. I just walked out to the car, with Maryjane trailing after me."

I said, "That was on Thursday. You checked yourself in on Saturday?"

"Yeah."

"Why did you come back then?"

"I came back because I couldn't stop cutting."

"So you cut yourself even more, after you left here on Thursday?"

"Oh yeah, I cut myself and I couldn't stop cutting. This was ongoing. It was the only thing on my mind. I just couldn't stop. I'd start with a superficial cut, then I'd get deeper and deeper, and I knew I wasn't going to quit. I was getting really worried, so I called Maryjane up, and she said it was better to voluntarily go in than to be committed. So I called the doctor on call here—I actually knew him—and there was a bed open, so I went in. It was funny because on my way down here, I was like kind of nervous, you know? I mean, I know where I'm heading, and I know I'm going to be here for a while, so I pulled in to a convenience store and bought the biggest beer they had and drank it. I thought, If I am going to have to wait three to five hours to be admitted, I am going to have a buzz."

Maryjane came back with a cheeseburger and fries, which brightened Anissa's mood. She told Anissa that she'd talked to the security guard about the Taco Bell food and that everything that happened was all just a big misunderstanding. "Anissa, he was just doing his job," she said, her voice firm yet compassionate. Anissa accepted what she said.

Presently a member of the Shoal Creek staff came into the room and told Anissa that it was time for therapy, and he told Maryjane and me that the visiting period was over. Anissa, Maryjane, and I walked to the front desk, where Maryjane and I signed out. We hugged Anissa and left her in a brighter mood than the one she'd been in when we arrived.

. . . . .

A few weeks later, Anissa and I got together on a Sunday afternoon at the Sports Performance International offices in the Arboretum area of northwest Austin. We'd spent many hours here over the previous year, usually on weekends, recording her story. So it was familiar turf.

Since I'd last seen her, she left Shoal Creek, made a transition into day therapy, and returned to her job part-time. Her meds were working, and she was looking for a therapist to complement the work of her psychiatrist. She looked the healthiest I'd seen her in a long time.

The group therapy she'd been doing during the days had been

helpful, not so much because it provided an avenue for her to bring up her own issues, which she did on some occasions, but because her listening to other patients discuss their issues gave her insight into herself: "I can't say how it works, but you listen and it makes you aware of what you're doing. Like one week the members of the group were talking about emotional regulation. What that is, it's like instead of going from zero to sixty with your emotions, you catch yourself. Put on the brakes before you max out. Because that's when the trouble really begins, when you let yourself go all the way to the maximum. You have to talk yourself down. That made so much sense to me, because I've seen myself do that, *wham!*, zero to sixty and I'm out of control.

"So there was this one day when I was aware of what was going on with me emotionally. I went into the bathroom and I actually did it. I talked myself down. I felt successful, because I'd quieted myself down instead of going nuts. Another thing you do, you call someone, just to talk. There are a lot of us in group who are cutters, and a lot of the time, it's an impulse thing. So if you do some emotional regulation when you feel that urge, it can stop you from cutting. It doesn't always take a long time. I did that once. I had this impulse to cut, so I called Dr. Spears and said, 'Hey, can you talk for about five minutes?' Then we just talked about our dogs for a few minutes. We didn't go into anything serious, but that's not what it's about. It's to give you a few minutes to get beyond the impulse."

We talked about the demon she mentioned earlier. Just as it would in her younger days, the demon had manifested itself as a very real being to her: "I realized he was back when I started cutting myself again. It was almost like when I did that I was feeding him, you know? He just came up to me and started telling me what a shitty person I was. After sleeping all that time, here he was, all full of energy and ready to rock 'n' roll again. He's just the ugliest demon ever, hanging out in my room, smoking a joint, just having a good ol' time and laughing at me." At Shoal Creek, Anissa had told the hospital therapists about the demon and they suggested she was hearing voices. No, she protested, it's not like that; it's different. Finally one social worker got it and told Anissa that what she was doing was a tried-and-true psychological coping technique called splitting. Anissa explained: "It's what you do when there's such a horrendous part of yourself that you can't accept it as being part of you. It's easier for you to visualize it as something apart from you. So I picture it as a demon and I can think of it as not me. You know, you can't hate yourself that much, so you put it off as something else. Getting that perspective on it really helped me."

As she thought back over the past few months, she told me that all the bad stuff she'd been through had value: She said she'd learned, once and for all, that the old ways of reacting to stressful events would not work.

. . . . .

As we talked, I felt encouraged about the progress Anissa had made at Shoal Creek and during the weeks following her release. That didn't mean I thought everything was perfect for her. In fact, it was obvious to me that the road ahead for her would be fraught with difficult turns. There would always be a very real possibility that at some point she'd trip and fall so hard that she would not be able to pick herself up and get back on track. But my bets would be on her succeeding. Anissa has fortitude in abundance.

When we started our collaboration, Anissa said she wanted to write a book that would speak to all women, but in particular to young Hispanic women. The message: You don't have to feel limited in your choices. You can achieve things. You can do more than have babies and make tortillas, if you have a mind to. Anissa's two world boxing championships would stand as testament to that verity.

But as we depart the office building and walk out into the resplendent sunshine of a perfect autumn afternoon in Texas, I'm thinking Anissa is about much more than attaining dreams. In fact, forget dreams. Anissa's great accomplishment is just being alive and able to function in the world, given the travails she's dealt with since she was seven years old. Living well is not only the best revenge, it's also the greatest success, I'm thinking. And maybe that's the most important message to learn from Anissa's story.

Her lifetime record in the ring ended up at 17-14-2. A winning record, to be sure, but not an overly notable one if you just consider the numbers. One significant thing about her career was she was never once knocked out; maybe it's the most significant thing. True, she came close with that late-career TKO; nevertheless, it wasn't a knockout. I'm thinking now that her boxing career is nothing if not a reflection of the bigger picture of her life. Sure, she had some defeats along the way, but she never got knocked out in life either. At the end, she was always on her feet.

We chat outside for a while longer, and then it's time to leave. I walk toward my small SUV, but think of one last thing I want to say. So I turn back to her.

"You're tough!" I call to Anissa as she's climbing into her car.

She doesn't hear me. She opens the car door. "Huh?" she shouts.

"You're tough!" I repeat.

This time she gets it. I doubt that you can pay her a greater compliment. Anissa's distinctive girlish smile spreads across her face, and she starts her engine to head out on the road.

. . . . .

A few weeks later, Anissa returned to the boxing gym and began training. Early on, she put herself through light routines. Then she began to push herself more. But she was cautious. If her shoulder or her knee began to bother her, she'd back off, maybe stay away from the gym for a few days, then return and pick up the intensity once more. Though she confessed to being burdened with a lot of ring rust, her native athleticism shined as she exhibited her mastery of the double-end bags or shadowboxed.

After a while, she began to speculate about whether she could actually make a comeback as a pro. That old dream of fighting for a WBC title never fully went away, and one day she confessed to me that she'd just about convinced herself to take a stab at fighting again. But various aches and strains soon reminded Anissa of her age and what all her body had been through. I didn't see her for a week or two, and when we talked next, she told me she'd put the WBC dream back in the closet.

While I never doubted that she could make a valiant effort to return to the ring, I was glad she decided it wasn't the right thing to do. Recently a mutual friend of ours who had been a terrifically gifted boxer as a young man attempted to press his career onward even though he was now in his forties. I watched at ringside one night as a much younger fighter destroyed him and his career. I hated to think Anissa might face the same sort of destruction.

The question of reviving her career resolved, Anissa nonetheless remained a gym regular, training hard for the sake of training hard. One day she donned her protective gear and climbed into the ring to spar for a few rounds, and she told me afterward she planned to keep on sparring. I was happy to hear that, for sparring brings a kind of reward you can't get from just working out. I thought it could help her keep her demons at bay. So it was good to see her sparring, and it was good to see her training other women in the gym. It was good to shoot the shit with her during workout breaks and it was good to hear her distinct laugh above the chatter of the speed bags and the buzzing of the round clocks. Her mental state improved to the point that she was able to stop using psychotropic meds altogether. On top of that, she was getting along well with her family, especially her mother: "I see my mother now for who she is. I wouldn't want her any different."

Just past dawn one Saturday, I pulled into the parking lot outside Richard's gym. As I climbed out of my car, I noticed the statue of Anissa was back on the roof, grinning into the gentle early morning sun, rejuvenated with fresh paint and other repairs. I smiled when I saw the statue. It belongs there.